HMS Hood

I dedicate this book
to the officers and men of HMS *Hood*,
and to all who fought for freedom.

HMS HOOD
PRIDE OF THE ROYAL NAVY

by
Andrew Norman

SPELLMOUNT
Staplehurst

Published in the United Kingdom in 2002 by
SPELLMOUNT LIMITED
The Old Rectory
Staplehurst, Kent TN12 0AZ

ISBN 1-86227-152-6

Published in the United States in 2001 by
Stackpole Books

A catalogue record of this book is available from the
British Library

1 3 5 7 9 8 6 4 2

MANUFACTURED IN THE UNITED STATES OF AMERICA

ACKNOWLEDGMENTS

I AM IMMENSELY GRATEFUL TO THE FOLLOWING FOR HELP, ADVICE, the sharing of reminiscences, and the loan of photographs: Her Majesty, the Queen; from the Royal Navy, Adm. Sir Henry Leach, Rear Adm. D. G. Spickernell, Vice Adm. Louis Le Bailly*, Rear Adm. M. Morgan-Giles, Rear Adm. Edward Gueritz, Cdr. G. A. G. Brooke, Lt. Cdr. Cedric C. Wake-Walker, Lady Anne Wake-Walker, Lt. Cdr. Peter Hay, Lt. Cdr. I. M. P. Coombes, Lt. Cdr. C. B. Kennedy, CPO Willam Stone*, Ted Briggs*, Fred White (founder, HMS *Hood* Association)*, John R. Williams (chairman, HMS *Hood* Association)*, George Bradford Jackson, CPO W. Harold Ransom*, John W. Hawthorne, Les Egerton, and E. Hephen; from the Royal Naval Volunteer Reserve, Capt. Ian Quarrie (Retd.)*, Lt. Cdr. J. Mercer, Lt. Cdr. G. H. Draysey, Lt. Cdr. William Kentish, and Lt. Robin Board*; and from the Royal Air Force, Sgt. Thomas McLaren.

Thanks also to Jeannie McLean, Rita Ainsworth, Hannah C. Snook, Jeanne Spacey, Joan Cherrison, Connie Halman, Joan Hill, Alice E. Reekie, Sonia M. Cooper, Meg Chapman, Joyce Cummins, Laura Annie Day, Jane Francis, Diane Benison, Yvonne Ransom, Heather Churcher, Jane Hay, Mary Tilburn, Anne Davidson, Melanie Bright (Features Editor of *Jane's Defence Weekly*), Jock Gardner (Naval Historical Branch), David K. Brown, Brian P. Constable, Arthur C. Wilson, David Fricker, Terry Parker, Robert Steel, Mike Reed, Gerry Senior (for the "Song of HMS *Hood*"), Martin Jackson, John Bushell (for loan of his father Frederick's Diary of the 1923–24 World Cruise), James Bradford, Brian Tilburn, Peter Devlin, John Hawthorne, John Guise, and Milo J. Kerr. Finally, thanks to the librarian and staff of Poole Central Library, Royal Naval Museum,

Royal Naval Submarine Museum, HMS *Excellent,* and the Dorset Fire and Rescue Service; editors of the *Times* newspaper, *Portsmouth News, Lymington Times, Navy News,* and *Jane's Defence Weekly;* the Reverend Malcolm Riches of the Church of St. John the Baptist, Boldre, Hampshire; and especially to Mary E. Hurst, for all her practical help and encouragement.

*Served on HMS *Hood.*

CONTENTS

Acknowledgments v
British Naval Terminology ix
"Song of HMS Hood*"* xi
Prologue xiii

Part One. *Life of a Ship* 1

   1. Welcome Aboard HMS *Hood* 3

   2. Recollections of a Crew Member 9

   3. Recollections of a Midshipman 19

   4. Recollections of a Captain's Messenger 25

   5. Recollections of a Signalman 29

   6. Recollections of a Midshipman Who Steered *Hood* 35

   7. Recollections of an Engineer Artificer:
      Hood's World Cruise 37

Part Two. *Death of a Ship* 49

   8. The Stage Is Set 51

   9. The British Fleet 63

  10. Into Battle 79

  11. *Hood* Goes Down 91

  12. *Prince of Wales* Fights On 101

  13. The End of *Bismarck* 107

Part Three. *The Postmortem* **111**
   14. The Boards of Enquiry 113
   15. Vice Admiral Holland's Tactics 117

Part Four. *The Enduring Mystery of* Hood's *Loss* **125**
   16. Doubts over the Official Verdict 127
   17. Other Possible Causes 131
   18. Conclusion 141

   Appendix A: The Search for the Sunken Bismarck
              and Hood 147
   Appendix B: A Strange Coincidence 151
   Bibliography 153
   Index 155

BRITISH NAVAL TERMINOLOGY

On a ship, *port* is left (red) and *starboard* right (green) when facing forward.

Bearings and courses are given in degrees, north being 000° and south 180°.

One *knot* equals one nautical mile per hour, a nautical mile being equal to 1.15 miles.

On the bow means that another vessel or object is lying in an area between right ahead and 90°, and *on the quarter* means that it is lying between 90° and right astern.

A lookout referring to an enemy ship may signal, "Alarm starboard green 45°." This means that the vessel he has sighted is on the starboard side, and its direction, taken from the way his own ship is facing, is 45°. (Binoculars other than hand-held ones were calibrated especially for this purpose.)

Divisions are parades for inspection by the inspecting divisional officer.

The day and night are divided into periods called *watches*. These include *middle* (early morning), *morning, forenoon, afternoon, first dog* (early evening), and *last dog* (late evening).

A and *B* refer to the forward turrets; *X* and *Y* to those aft.

The *arcs of fire* are the relative bearings over which the guns of a ship can be brought to bear without being obstructed by the ship's own superstructure. *A* arcs are the bearings over which the greatest proportion of the main armament bears.

"SONG OF HMS *HOOD*"

THIS SONG WAS SUNG BY SAILORS IN PUBLIC HOUSES IN THE
Portsmouth area after the sinking of HMS *Hood*, to the tune of
"Silent Night."

In Scapa Flow she lay, HMS Hood,
Pride of them all, awaiting the call;
Proud, oh so proud, of her fifteen-inch guns
Fearing not the arrogant Huns.

Resting in sunshine and peace,
Resting in sunshine and peace.

Then orders they came— "Anchors aweigh!"
And slowly she slid from the Flow that day.
Atlantic patrol was ordered—Take care!
Bismarck *was sighted, but do not know where.*

All guns were ordered to load,
All guns were ordered to load.

Then came the moment for her guns to play
When Bismarck *was sighted that day in May.*
But fate played her hand and the old Dreadnought
From stem to stern her timbers were wrought;

And her men were flung far and wide,
Into a mountainous sea.

Then came George the Fifth, *the* Rodney *as well;*
Vengeance was sought with powder and shell.
Norfolk *and* Suffolk, *they joined in the fray;*
Bismarck *was doomed and could not slip away*

She was sunk and gone for all time,
Sunk and gone for all time.

Now sweethearts and wives, and mother be proud,
Proud of your sons defending their flag.
Good men died fighting for Britain and you
Can be proud, oh so proud, of the red, white, and blue.

May God rest their souls in peace,
Rest them in heavenly peace.

PROLOGUE

As the mighty battle cruiser HMS *Hood* sank into the icy depths of the Atlantic Ocean on May 24, 1941, she took with her the lives of 1,418 brave men—and a secret that has haunted the maritime world ever since.

HMS *Hood* seemed invincible, and the hopes of the British Navy in wartime had rested on her broad image. She was the one vessel that Britain relied upon to match the enemy ~~pocket~~ battleships such as *Bismarck*.

Her tragic demise was greeted with disbelief by the nation, and the shock waves reverberated all around the world. Suddenly Britain at sea seemed very vulnerable.

This powerful and graceful ship, which epitomized British naval power, was sunk a mere seven minutes after engaging the *Bismarck* and her consort, the cruiser *Prinz Eugen*. Her colossal size, 48,360 tons fully loaded and 860 feet in length, and her armament, which included eight 15-inch and eight 4-inch guns, did not save her.

The following pages relate the experiences of some of those who were engaged directly or indirectly with *Hood,* both in her prewar days and on her final journey. This voyage began in the early hours of the morning of May 22. At 6 A.M. on May 24, she broke in two and sank to the bottom of the sea, taking most of her complement of 95 officers and 1,326 men with her. Although only three men survived *Hood's* sinking, others are still alive who spent time aboard the mighty ship in the years before that fateful day in May 1941.

Hood *entering harbor in Malta, her "B" turret painted red, white, and blue signifying her neutrality in the Spanish Civil War.* FRED WHITE

This book has been written to honor HMS *Hood* and to pay tribute to all who ever served aboard her, whether above or below decks. For that reason, the emphasis is not so much on the recounting of historic events, such as the unrest at Invergordon in 1931 (a so-called mutiny that was precipitated when the sailors' wages were cut drastically, and which ended with the resignation of the first sea lord and the premature retirement of seven admirals and the captains of five capital ships) or the destruction of the French fleet at Mers-el-Kebir in 1940. These things have appeared in many works before. Instead, it is based on personal stories that highlight the special character of the "Mighty *Hood*" and those who were privileged to be part of her complement.

During the extensive research conducted for this book, which included sources such as German naval records of the battle, one glaring discrepancy kept surfacing that puzzled me. Finally I came up with a theory as to why *Hood* sank, one that has not been explored before. After taking all the evidence into account, I recalled the words of Sherlock Holmes: "When you have eliminated the impossible, whatever remains, however improbable, must be the truth."

Church of St. John the Baptist, Boldre. AUTHOR'S PHOTO

Boldre Church,
Book of Remembrance.

REV. MALCOLM RICHES

No official memorial was erected to HMS *Hood,* but in the peaceful atmosphere of the Church of St. John the Baptist at Boldre in the New Forest of Hampshire, she is remembered once a year on a Sunday in May when relatives and friends of those who died, as well as those who previously served on *Hood,* come to the church to worship and pay their respects.

In the porch are two Vice-Admiral's lanterns and two long oak benches carved with the ship's badge depicting a Cornish chough and an anchor. A painting of *Hood* by eminent marine artist Montague Dawon hangs in the North Chapel. In the corner, directly opposite the entrance, is a book containing the names of all 1,418 officers and men of the ship's company who were lost. A small stained glass window depicts St. Nicholas, patron saint of sailors.

PART ONE

Life of a Ship

CHAPTER 1

Welcome Aboard
HMS *Hood*

A VISITOR TO HMS *HOOD* IN THE 1920S RECEIVED A SMALL booklet printed by Charpentier Ltd. of Portsmouth, from which he or she would have gleaned the following information about the great ship.

HMS *Hood* was the largest, heaviest, and fastest armored warship in the world, at 860 feet long, with a beam of 104 feet, a draught of 32$^{1}/_{2}$ feet, a displacement of 44,600 tons, and a maximum speed of 32 knots. Three times around the ship was 1 mile.

Building of *Hood* began on September 1, 1916, at John Brown and Company's shipyard on Clydebank. She was launched two years later, on August 22, 1918, by Lady Hood, widow of Rear Adm. Horace Lambert Hood, who lost his life at the Battle of Jutland in his ship HMS *Invincible*. Over the following nineteen months, *Hood* was fitted out and, on March 29, 1920, was finally commissioned. Her original cost was £6,025,000 ($9,037,500).

At the foremast, the ship normally flew the flag of the admiral commanding the battle cruiser squadron. On the ship's crest, depicting an anchor and a Cornish chough, were emblazoned the Latin words *Ventis Secundus*, meaning "With Favorable Winds." She was

Laying down of HMS Hood, *the longest ship built for the Navy. John Brown's shipyard, Clydebank, September 1916.* R. N. MUSEUM

named after the family of Hoods who have provided England with some of her greatest sailors, among them Viscount Samuel Hood, who brought the French to action in the West Indies at the close of the eighteenth century.

In wartime, she had a complement of about fourteen hundred officers and men, but in peacetime only twelve hundred. Her officers included navigators, gunners, engineers, paymasters, wireless operators, naval instructors, schoolmasters, and midshipmen. Besides seamen and engine-room artificers, there were shipwrights, joiners, coopers, painters, plumbers, sailmakers, blacksmiths, coppersmiths, fitters and turners, enginesmiths, bootmakers, cooks, butchers, postmen, waiters, and servants, as well as 199 Royal marines. Her monthly payroll averaged about £6,000 ($9,000).

The ship was virtually a village in herself. *Hood* carried in her storerooms provisions sufficient for four months—about 320 tons—including fresh meat for one month in her refrigerator. A normal breakfast for the ship's company consisted of four sides of bacon, 300

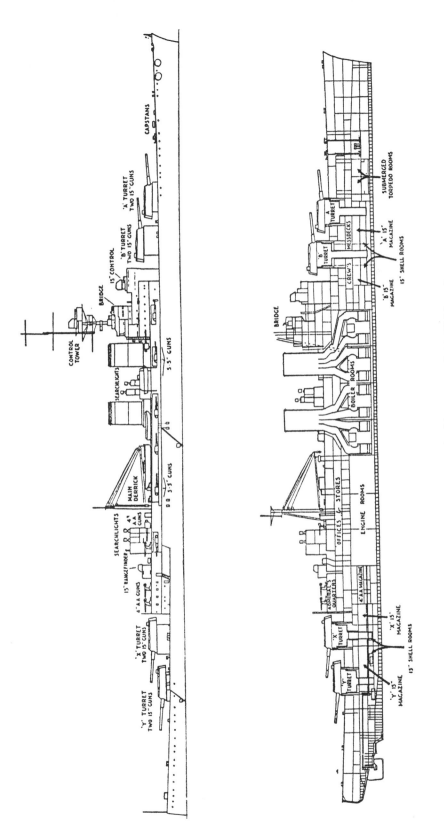

Sectional drawings from the blueprints of HMS Hood.

pounds of tomatoes, 100 gallons of tea, 600 pounds of bread, and 75 pounds of butter. Those aboard could purchase groceries from the canteen. If uniforms needed to be altered or shoes or boots mended, a rating would act as tailor or cobbler in his spare time. There was also a bookshop onboard.

Medical facilities included a sick bay with general and isolation wards, an operating room, an X-ray department, and a dispensary. Medical personnel included two doctors, a dentist, and a trained staff.

Below the quarterdeck was the chapel, dedicated to Our Lady and St. Nicholas, which was used for holy communion, evensong, and daily services. Parade services, however, were held on the quarterdeck or, in bad weather, on the mess decks.

The ship carried three steamboats, four motorboats, and eleven sailing and pulling boats, as well as more than enough Carley floats (emergency rafts) and life buoys to support the rest of the ship's company in case the ship had to be abandoned.

Two hundred or so electric fans pumped air through ventilation trunks to supply the living and working spaces. There were 3,874 electric light fittings and six large searchlights, each of 120 million candlepower, as well as several smaller ones fitted with shutters for flashing messages. The nearly 200 miles of permanent electric cable weighed about 100 tons. Three hundred eighty telephones operated through one main exchange and several subexchanges.

The main engines of the ship consisted of four complete Brown Curtis geared turbine units, each driving a 20-ton propeller through some 300 feet of shafting. Thirty auxiliary machinery rooms housed dynamos, pumps, and other machinery, the total weight of which was over 5,000 tons. Four boiler rooms, which could be reached by electric lifts, held twenty-four oil burning Yarrow boilers. *Hood* ran on oil, and her fuel tanks had a capacity of 4,600 tons.

Her main armament consisted of eight 15-inch guns, set in pairs in revolving turrets and capable of an elevation of 30 degrees. Each

Wardroom. In accordance with tradition the officers remained seated for loyal toasts. FRED WHITE

Seamen's Mess. FRED WHITE

turret with its twin guns weighed 900 tons yet was so finely balanced that it moved noiselessly. Each shell weighed 1,920 pounds, required a propelling charge of 640 pounds of cordite, and left the muzzle at a speed of 1,670 miles per hour. The maximum height of a shell in flight exceeded the height of Mont Blanc (15,772 feet), and the shell would destroy a target at a range of 30,000 yards. Sixty-four men were required to work one gun turret, and all the guns could be controlled and fired electrically from the control tower. The ship also had twelve 5.5-inch guns, six on each side; four 4-inch long-range antiaircraft guns; numerous automatic guns for dealing with aircraft at short range; and two submerged and four above-water torpedo tubes. Each torpedo cost over £2,000 ($3,000).

As a defense against torpedoes, *Hood* had protective bulges below the waterline and was fitted with 13,800 tons of armor, that on the hull being twelve inches thick.

CHAPTER 2

Recollections
of a Crew Member

As I sat opposite former *Hood* crew member Fred White in his sitting room, it was hard to believe that this spritely and smartly dressed gentleman could have served on HMS *Hood* in 1937 and 1938; he simply did not look old enough. Talking about his experiences on the mighty ship so many years later, he was still visibly moved.

White shared the feelings of many a seagoing man in the war whose life had been saved by a change of draft. Fate had taken him away from *Hood* before her final tragic journey, but this only intensified his grief for those who had died. Recalling the moment he learned that his old ship was lost, he said, "A friend with me on board HMS *Penelope* had just read the notice that had been posted: '*Hood* lost.' I felt as though a piece of me had gone down with her."

Although he was spared the agony of *Hood,* he survived the sinking of HMS *Dainty* and explained just how painful it was to watch a ship go down: "You watch your whole world disappearing before your eyes. Everything you own, everything that has been your life— your letters, clothes, personal effects—are snatched away by the sea.

Fred White, new entry, Royal Naval Barracks, Portsmouth, 1936.

FRED WHITE

Battle-cruiser HMS Hood *seen from astern.* FRED WHITE

Emperor Haile Selassie of Ethiopia aboard HMS Hood. FRED WHITE

All you are left with is what you are wearing." He described the hollow screams and echoes of the tortured metal of a dying ship being wrenched apart as the worst sounds a sailor can ever hear. It is deafening, the sound carrying for miles. The ship gasps its last breath as the water reaches the boilers and they release a hiss of steam.

The days before the war were very different for the crew of HMS *Hood*. She was the pride of Britain and the envy of other nations. The ship "showed the flag" all around the world, calling at many exotic ports, such as Honolulu, Tahiti, Samoa, Rio de Janeiro, and Trinidad. In some places, when no berth could be found large enough to accommodate her great size, she was obliged to anchor offshore. She was the largest ship to negotiate the Panama Canal, with a mere 18 inches of clearance on either side of the locks. As she passed through the main canal cuttings, where the cliffs were up to 200 feet in height, she had to move slowly to avoid causing a landslide.

During the twenties and thirties, there were parties and dancing on board, with the Royal Marine band playing on the quarterdeck beneath a great awning. *Hood* played host to royalty and dignitaries from many countries, including the emperor of Ethiopia and the king and queen of Norway.

Hood's crew was the first in the navy to be issued cups and saucers. Before that, naval crew members ate and drank out of bowls. Tablecloths made from white oilcloth replaced the cortiscene ones used on other ships. During those halcyon days, gunnery and torpedo exercises were almost forgotten; it was more important to have the ship shining with spit and polish to show her off to the world.

HMS *Hood* became a veritable Noah's Ark as she acquired a variety of pets, some given as gifts, on her travels. One of the ship's mascots, a goat, suffered a prank when of one of the ratings decided to push the poor animal through a skylight onto the admiral's bed. (It is unclear whether the admiral was in the bed at the time.) Also onboard was a wallaby, which had been presented to the ship at Freemantle. This animal liked to race the men along the deck. Hopping enthusiastically, it would forget to stop at the stern, and the men

One of Hood's *mascots entertains with a boxing bout.*   RITA AINSWORTH

would have to launch a picket boat to rescue it. Then there was the black beaver presented to Admiral Field at Calgary. This new crew member made his home on *Hood*'s boat deck. When in the tropics, the men slept on the deck and sometimes had quite a shock when they awoke to find the beaver cuddled up next to them. On a spring cruise in 1928, a racehorse, a donkey, a pair of flamingos, and a baby seal joined the crew.

Two of the most interesting creatures onboard were the cats, Ginger and Fishcake. Ginger was "top cat," as he was the older and stronger of the two. Much respected by the crew, he had lost a portion of his tail during an exercise when the ship was carrying out a full-caliber shoot. As was usual during such an exercise, the cats were

Hood's *cats* "Ginger" *and* "Fishcake." FRED WHITE

rounded up and placed in a wash deck locker out of harm's way. When the firing was over, however, a seaman lifted the iron lid of the locker, unaware that Ginger was inside. As the cat scrambled out, the sailor was so startled that he dropped the lid, and poor Ginger lost part of his tail.

Ginger adopted the crew, rather than the other way round. He picked three special friends out of the entire ship's company, which numbered nearly two thousand men. One of his special friends was the marine butcher, who always gave him choice cuts of meat. Then there was the able seaman who looked after his sanitary arrangements and changed his sand tray. Perhaps the cleverest choice of all, though, was the captain as his special friend, which gained him access to the captain's day cabin, a real privilege.

Ginger was always the first ashore after *Hood* had secured alongside a dockyard wall. As soon as the quarterdeck brow (gang plank) had been put out, off he went, and strange as it may seem, he never missed the ship's departure.

Animals were not the only strange acquisitions to find their way aboard *Hood*. On one occasion, a Rolls-Royce was hoisted onto the ship. The crew was bringing a motorbike with sidecar onboard as

Exercises. Aircraft from aircraft carrier Furious *"attacking"* Hood.
FRED WHITE

well when the commander, Arthur John Power, arrived on the scene. "What the hell is that? Take it off my ship!" he shouted. So the men unloaded the motorbike back onto the dock. The owner, a commissioned gunner nicknamed Clickety Click, started up the bike in a fit of pique and ran it over the dockside. Many years later, the motorbike reappeared, having become entangled in some wires when a ship was berthing.

The exercises carried out by *Hood* also provided quite a bit of excitement at times. On one occasion, while the ship was engaged in full-power trials in the North Sea with the admiral of the fleet, Lord Jellicoe, onboard, she caused quite a stir. As *Hood* tore through the sea at 33 knots, plumes of water were forced up through the three hawse pipes high into the air. *Hood*'s siren jammed open, the ear-splitting sound seeming to fill the North Sea. A prolonged blast in naval language means "I'm in distress," so this caused much consternation among the other battle cruisers taking part in the exercise.

Panic ensued while the engineers tried to fix the problem, which took a long time. *Hood*'s bearings subsequently ran hot, which slowed her speed considerably, but she still made port at Invergordon with the rest of the fleet.

Another incident occurred when the battle cruisers left Invergordon for a practice 15-inch shoot, but this time the effect was more personal. As the cease-fire sounded, Chief Cook Fred Grant went up on deck, believing the firing to be safely concluded. But a gun in one turret had had a misfire, and the safety routine in such an event was for the gun's crew to go through a misfire drill and fire the gun. The force of the blast blew all the gilt buttons off poor Fred's petty officer's coat and made him permanently deaf in his left ear.

On a later cruise in 1934, HMS *Hood* and HMS *Renown* were engaged in exercises when *Renown* rammed *Hood* on her starboard quarter abreast of X turret. The damage necessitated both ships being dry-docked, and Admiral Bailey of *Hood* and Captain Sawbridge of *Renown* faced courts-martial. Both eventually were acquitted. Earlier, *Hood* had narrowly avoided a collision with a submarine, whose coxswain froze during exercises and was unable to follow orders. Her captain, with great presence of mind, took over and managed to dive his submarine just before she was hit by *Hood*.

In June 1931, *Hood* left Portsmouth after an extensive refit. She had been recommissioned and fitted with catapult-airplane-launching gear. Her decks were severely congested, however, and the only site that could be found for this to be installed was on the quarterdeck. Because *Hood*'s stern was so low in the water, the aircraft was washed away soon afterward when the ship was crossing the Atlantic.

On another cruise, a boy seaman was discovered missing after the ship had left Gibraltar and was headed south into the Atlantic. A court of enquiry ruled that he had been lost at sea. *Hood* later returned to the spot where it was believed the boy had been lost, and the crew held a memorial service, firing guns in salute and dropping wreaths into the water. A few years later, one of the chief stokers was visiting Sydney, Australia. Entering a pub, he couldn't believe his eyes. There before him was the missing boy, who had not been washed overboard at all, but jumped ship at Gibraltar and joined his brother on a merchant ship, where he became a stowaway, eventually reaching Sydney and settling down.

Fred White remembers with great affection every detail of his time onboard, even the time when he had to clean out *Hood's* oil tanks while she was in dock. It was an eerie task, the only light being at the end of a long, trailing lead that he clutched tightly as he crawled through the empty tanks on hands and knees, scooping up the oil slush in buckets. It was hardly worth the extra sixpence he was paid per day for doing this, but despite all the discomfort, he had the satisfaction of knowing that he was one of only a very few men who had ever gone into the bowels of the ship.

By all accounts, *Hood* was a ship to be reckoned with, her scrubbed decks and polished brass attesting to the fact that she was pride of the British Navy. With her sad demise, many a sailor's heart sank with her. She had been a great ship to serve on and had led her crew into many an adventure, leaving them with fond memories tinged with sadness. Thanks to the loyalty and hard work of founder Fred White, HMS *Hood* Association has gathered many photographs, mementos, and memories as an epitaph to the mighty ship.

CHAPTER 3

Recollections of a Midshipman

Ian Quarrie, probationary midshipman on Hood, *in naval "Whites."*

IAN QUARRIE

MIDSHIPMAN IAN QUARRIE, OF THE ROYAL NAVAL VOLUNTEER Reserve (RNVR), relished the danger of being swung violently in the "spotting top" high above the deck of HMS *Hood* as she rolled 40 degrees one way, righted herself, and then rolled 40 degrees the other in the force 12 gale. He loved heights, and bracing himself against the wind and rain, he peered into the squall, keeping a sharp lookout as midshipman of the watch. The storm was so fierce that the heavy oak wardroom table, which normally seated eighty officers, overturned, smashing all the crockery. But this did not deter the young naval officer.

Quarrie had loved the sea ever since his father had taken him aboard the Cunard liners that he captained. He remembered vividly being bathed in the washbasin in his father's cabin onboard one of those luxury ships. He also got to visit the engine room and other "forbidden" areas.

The seed was sown within him, and despite studying law at London University and working in a solicitor's office while in training, he went to sea as soon as an opportunity arose.

Quarrie had joined the RNVR and been appointed to HMS *President* on the Victoria Embankment for training on July 9, 1938, a year before war broke out. For a time he managed to cope with this along with his law studies. However, once the Navy started recruiting for the war from the RNVR, stating that anyone who was prepared to serve for a continuous six-month period would be sure of a commission to the next highest rank, Quarrie realized that he could be promoted quickly to sublieutenant, and the temptation was too great. He abandoned his law studies and signed up for six months.

He was sent out to Malta to join HMS *Shropshire,* a county class cruiser. He enjoyed his time aboard immensely, and during this period he became runner for the admiral, Commander-in-Chief Mediterranean. About two months into training, however, he learned that HMS *Hood* would be calling into Malta on her way home to Portsmouth. If only he could arrange a transfer to *Hood,* he thought, he would be able to serve on the most famous ship in the Navy.

The day that HMS *Hood* entered Grand Harbour, Malta, is one that Quarrie will never forget. "She looked absolutely beautiful," he says. He immediately asked his senior officer if a transfer might be possible. As luck would have it, HMS *Hood* had arranged that once in Malta, some of her midshipmen would leave and six or seven others would be taken onboard in order to take the navigation exam that would enable them to be promoted to sublieutenant. Here was Quarrie's golden opportunity.

Hood *alongside South Mole at Gibraltar.* FRED WHITE

The first thing the young midshipman noticed was the friendliness that extended to all levels—she was a happy ship. A fully ranked captain, H. T. C. "Hookey" Walker, was in charge, and according to Quarrie, he was a magnificent captain. Captain Walker had lost a hand in World War I in Zeebrugge and had a hook in its place, earning him his nickname. This appliance came into its own one day when the captain asked the young midshipman to open a window for him. The window was stuck fast, and strain as he might, Quarrie could not open it. The captain leaped to his feet, and with one mighty wrench with his hook, he rendered the window wide open.

After two short trial periods on *Hood* while he still officially belonged to HMS *Shropshire,* Quarrie finally transferred permanently, and for the next four months and the journey home to England, he served aboard HMS *Hood.* Quarrie found that on a ship the size of *Hood,* some of the duties that had been required of him on the smaller *Shropshire* were no longer his—tasks such as having to brew cocoa during the night watches, which was now the duty of the leading torpedo man.

As a midshipman, he did not share the wardroom for meals, since this was for senior officers. Instead, he and his fellow midshipmen and sublieutenants ate in the gunroom and were known as gunroom officers. They were, however, allowed to drink in the wardroom. He shared sleeping quarters with about twelve other midshipmen, but at least on HMS *Hood* they all had bunks, rather than the hammocks they might be expected to use onboard other vessels. The food was good, particularly in harbor, but Quarrie remembers the good comradeship most fondly.

A few things about *Hood* were in sharp contrast with HMS *Shropshire* and the other county class cruisers. For one, *Hood* had two steam picket boats of the brass-funnel type, which were far more interesting to run than *Shropshire's* 35-foot motorboats.

Surprisingly, the hot water arrangements for *Hood* were more outdated than those of *Shropshire*. The gunroom bathroom had an antiquated hot water system whereby cold water passed into a tank, and then steam was passed through the water to heat it. This method meant that only a limited quantity of hot water was available at a time, so Quarrie had many cold baths.

On one occasion when he was appointed as midshipman of the watch, Quarrie made his mark by suggesting during a fierce gale that the ship could go faster. He had noticed that although the ship's engines were making revolutions for 4 knots, she was being blown backward at a rate of 4 knots. Since he was responsible to the lieutenant commander on watch, he reported this and said he was sure that *Hood* could manage 8 knots and thereby make headway. The lieutenant commander said that if that is what he thought, then he should call the captain and tell him so. Nervously, the young officer raised the receiver linking to the captain's telephone. "Midshipman Quarrie here, sir," he said, voice trembling. "Midshipman who?" came the gruff reply. "I don't think that's the right name, do you?" Quarrie said, "Sorry, sir. I mean midshipman of the watch." To his delight, the captain agreed with his suggestion and gave him permis-

Hood *on patrol 1939, seen from the French battle cruiser Dunkerque.*
ALICE E. REEKIE

sion to ring down the new instructions to the engine room, so he was responsible for *Hood's* change of speed and progress.

It was at times like these, when storms raged, that the officers used the closed bridge of *Hood*. This was situated below the main bridge, which was open to the elements and therefore unsuitable in rough weather.

On the journey home, Quarrie's action station was situated in X turret, where, during exercises, he would take up his position along with the other fifteen men with whom he shared it. There was only one man senior to himself present, and that was a lieutenant commander. Once battened down inside, the men could neither hear nor see anything, nor were they aware of the gun turret rotating. The only noise that penetrated was the muffled sound of their own gun as it went off.

On arrival back at Portsmouth, Quarrie changed out of uniform ready to go ashore. He opened a door to go out on deck to see what was happening, when the commander's voice rang out: "Will the officer in plus fours kindly get off the quarterdeck!"

While docked in Portsmouth, Quarrie had an opportunity to visit HMS *Renown,* which was undergoing a refit and was "in rather a mess." He noted in his log that "she has been fitted with two perpendicular, stream-lined and very tall funnels, which though they look admirable in the 'Arethusa' class of cruiser, do not suit *Renown's* style of beauty at all. Her Queen Anne's mansions [the name irreverently given by the sailors to the control tower because it resembled a block of flats in London of the same name] look a very clean and well protected job of work. But in spite of all this modernity, her 15" guns are STILL not fitted with anti-flash doors to the cordite hoists." Quarrie was pleased to note that at least HMS *Hood* had this protection.

Before leaving *Hood,* Midshipman Quarrie took the navigation exams he had worked so hard toward. When the results came out, the wait seemed interminable. The other seven regular officers received theirs first, and then the navigation officer turned to him and said, "Midshipman Quarrie—I don't think *Hood* is anywhere near the Sahara Desert do you?" He then apologized because he had been reading the coordinates that Quarrie had given him back to front. Quarrie did pass and received promotion to sublieutenant.

CHAPTER 4

Recollections of a Captain's Messenger

Charles Kennedy, Captain's Messenger, in March 1940 (after his transfer from Hood *to the Fleet Air Arm in April 1939).*

CHARLES KENNEDY

CHARLES BENJAMIN KENNEDY JOINED HMS *HOOD* IN 1938 AT age sixteen, a boy seaman. On *Hood,* he spent half of each day in classes, during which he got to know the ship. On one occasion, the gunnery warrant officer took the boy seamen down into the after 4-inch magazine and gave them a lecture. He stressed that a battle cruiser was never in any circumstances to engage an enemy battleship, because of the cruiser's lack of armor. His words were prophetic, and Kennedy never forgot them, because it was an explosion in this very magazine that was thought by some to be the cause of *Hood*'s tragic demise in May 1941.

Because he was an able boy who had performed well in his examinations, Kennedy was given accelerated promotion, first to ordinary seaman and then to captain's messenger. His job was now to dog the captain, H. T. C. "Hookey" Walker, whom he describes as "a splendid fellow," around the ship through all the working hours, making sure he did not omit to polish the captain's brass hook, which replaced the hand he had lost in World War I. In fact, the captain possessed two hooks, one for going ashore and the other for going to sea, the latter being adapted to hold a telescope.

The captain's Royal Marine servant would hang the captain's hook behind the door of his cabin, which was situated where its occupant could step directly out onto the quarterdeck and take his morning constitutional. On one occasion a young boy seaman who had just joined the ship and was therefore ignorant of protocol asked Kennedy if he might leave a note for the captain. The normal procedure would have been for him to make the request to his divisional officer, who would have sent it on to the commander and so on up the chain. However, the boy seaman simply showed Kennedy the note and asked, "What shall I do with this?" To which Kennedy replied, looking at the captain's hook, "Hang it up there!" When Captain Walker returned and discovered the note, he was most upset and a row ensued, in the course of which Kennedy thought it best to confess.

As was the custom in those days, the captain had his barge painted brightly in enamel paint with the appropriate colors and dressed his personal staff in matching, tailor-made suits. This was done at his own expense.

Every Sunday morning, the keyboard sentry, who kept guard outside the captain's cabin, carried two benches and the lectern out onto the quarterdeck for the morning service. It was Kennedy's task to polish these benches, which stood outside the cabin, with mansion polish while the captain worked inside at his desk. (These benches were considered a fire risk and therefore removed from HMS *Hood* before the war. They may now be seen in the porch of the Church of St. John the Baptist at Boldre, in the New Forest.) The keyboard sentry's job was to guard the keys to all the important rooms, as well as the glass-fronted case in which the keys to the ship's magazines were kept locked safely away.

Kennedy's action station was one of the 5.9-inch port-side guns, where he was a sight setter. The crew would fire these guns in the event that a destroyer attacked with torpedoes.

CHAPTER 5

Recollections
of a Signalman

Signalman W. H. Ransom
with searchlight. YVONNE RANSOM

"FLAG 18 BLUE—HOIST!" THE ORDER, CONVERTED INTO CODE BY
the leading signalman on the bridge, came down by speaking tube to
the flag deck, which was situated on the control tower just below the
admiral's bridge. At this time, the vice admiral commanding *Hood*
was A. B. "Cuts" Cunningham. Immediately Signalman W. H. Ransom selected the appropriate flag to be run up high on the masthead
above the compass platform. "Execute" came the order, and as the
flag was swiftly hauled down, *Hood* and her destroyer escort duly
turned together 180 degrees to port.

Hood *with* Repulse *and* Glorious, *spring maneuvers in Atlantic,
January 1938, Marine's gun crew.* FRED WHITE

Harold Ransom had joined the Navy in May 1934, and after fifteen months at the shore station HMS *Ganges* near Ipswich, reputedly
the toughest training school in the navy, he was sent to *Hood.* His pay
was then eight shillings and sixpence per week, which rose to the
princely sum of fourteen shillings per week when he was seventeen
and a half. As signal boy and later signalman, he quickly realized that
every movement of a ship, whether alone or in consort, was controlled by flags. He therefore had to know his flag signals by heart. If
the ship engaged the enemy, then every second would be vital.

There were forty signalmen on *Hood,* and so ingrained in them
was their knowledge of flags and signals that even when they were
marching, they did it by signals. "G10!" barked the leading signalman, meaning "quick march." There were code letters and numbers
for everything and everyone. Position "Q" was the position in which
the battle cruisers lined up, as in the case of a fleet review, and the
"A-K" line was the one taken up by the cruisers. "ACQ" meant
"admiral commanding *Hood*," and the code letter for a battle fleet
was "U."

Recovering Hood's *picket boat.* FRED WHITE

Ransom had only ever seen the fleet formed up once. Because the ships occupied an area of fifty square miles, the Mediterranean wasn't big enough, so they had to form up in the Atlantic. The lines and lines of ships stretched to the far horizon and beyond. Minesweepers, motor torpedo boats, submarines, the destroyer asdic (sonar) screen, light cruisers, heavy cruisers, aircraft carriers, and last of all, the mighty battle cruisers and battleships. With a fleet of this size, there was a great deal of practice in formation. Coordination and precision in maneuvering were essential if they were to avoid collisions. A good captain knew his signals as well as the signalmen did. There was some confusion, however, when they encountered merchant ships, as the Royal Navy used naval code and the Merchant Navy used the international code.

After a little less than two years, *Hood's* ship's company was paid off, and a largely new crew signed up. For Ransom, this meant a transfer to Malta, where the home fleet was based, to the Castile Signal Station, the headquarters of which was a large mansion dating to the tenth century. Six months later, he was back aboard *Hood*.

Harold Ransom served aboard HMS *Hood* when she was assigned to patrol the coast of Spain during the Spanish Civil War (1936–39), when General Franco and his nationalist "Insurgents" were attempting to overthrow the "Popular Front," a center-left alliance formed in 1931 when the Republic was established. Although the British government had a policy of nonintervention in Spain, the Royal Navy was assigned to deter any attempts to interfere with shipping on the high seas.

By April 1937, when Franco's forces had failed to take Madrid and were attacking the Basques and their northern Spanish port of Bilbao, an English entrepreneur nicknamed "Potato Jones" and others braved Franco's blockade to bring in English potatoes and other foodstuffs to the beleaguered inhabitants.

When the situation deteriorated, HMS *Hood* was dispatched from Gibraltar to reinforce British destroyers already in the area. It was here that the great ship—the ultimate deterrent—would have her way without having to fire a single shot.

Vice Admiral Sir Geoffrey Blake chose April 23, St. George's Day, to test the effectiveness of Franco's blockade of Bilbao by overseeing the safe passage of three English merchant ships, the *MacGregor, Hamsterley,* and *Stanbrook,* into that port from the nearby French port of St. Jean de Luz.

At 4:15 A.M., *Hood* sighted the three merchant ships on the horizon with the British destroyer *Firedrake* astern. She signaled the *Firedrake,* "Follow in and report immediately any action taken by Insurgents when merchant ships are outside territorial waters."

At 5:52 A.M., the insurgent cruiser *Almirante Cervera* came in sight, and at 6:30 A.M., the *MacGregor* signaled that an armed trawler had requested her to stop. Vice Admiral Blake then ordered *Firedrake,* "Proceed to *MacGregor* and warn armed trawler not to interfere outside territorial waters."

Almirante Cervera, which then proceeded to steam at high speed ahead of *Hood* toward the convoy of merchantmen, signaled *Firedrake,* "Please tell steamers not to enter Bilbao," whereupon *Hood* replied,

"Stop interfering." When *Almirante Cervera* protested to *Hood* that the "English ships are within six miles which are our territorial waters," *Hood* ignored her and signaled to the *MacGregor,* "Continue your voyage if you wish." *Firedrake* reported, "Trawler fired a round across bows of leading [merchant] vessel."

There then followed a protracted argument between the commanders of *Hood* and *Almirante Cervera,* the latter saying that his government observed a limit of six miles from the coast, and *Hood* insisting that "the British government does not recognize your jurisdiction outside three miles."

At 8:33 A.M., as *Firedrake* was escorting the merchant ships toward the three-mile limit, the British destroyer *Fortune* came in sight and promptly signaled to Blake, "*Cervera* has guns trained on merchant vessels." *Hood* responded by training her guns on *Almirante Cervera.* The outcome was that the Insurgents remained outside the three-mile limit, and all three merchant ships arrived safely in port, to a rapturous reception from the crowds. Blake signaled *Firedrake,* "Duty well executed," and *Fortune,* "I am sorry we could not provide you with more amusement."

CHAPTER 6

Recollections of a Midshipman Who Steered *Hood*

*Probationary midshipman
Robin Board on the deck of
HMS* Hood, *1934.* ROBIN BOARD

WHEN ROBIN BOARD OF HILL HEAD IN HAMPSHIRE WAS A PROBA-
tionary midshipman in the Royal Naval Volunteer Reserve (RNVR),
he once steered HMS *Hood*. He was an eighteen-year-old student of
architecture at the time, and the year was 1934. It was customary for
reserves to do one month of sea training annually, and *Hood* was his
first ship. The steering compartment was an octagonal structure situated on the control tower below the compass platform and the huge
rangefinder. He describes the event as follows:

The battle cruiser *Hood,* the most beautiful ship in the world, was
steaming up the Northumberland coast at 22 knots on a calm night.

It was partway through the middle watch. In the wheelhouse, a surprisingly small, dimly lit cell two-thirds of the way up the great steel citadel that formed her forward superstructure, an RNVR midshipman was at the wheel. The wheel wasn't very big, and it stood on a scrubbed beech grating. In front of him was a slit in the 12-inch armor, about 3 inches high and 3 feet wide. Through this, a narrow slice of gray sea alternated with gray sky as the bow gently rose and dipped.

But his eyes were glued to the green band above it, across which a series of numbers moved in staccato jerks. His job was to keep the pointer steadily on 330°, but it kept slipping off, and each time, the quartermaster beside him gently gave a turn or two to correct the swing.

After some time, he seemed to get the hang of it. At the first minute sign of movement, he would make three full turns of the wheel, and then perhaps twenty seconds later, when the swing in that direction was just discernible, he hastily made five turns in the opposite direction, gradually ironing out the pendulum effect of 3° of helm on 860 feet of ship. He could feel the deep heartbeat of her screws under his feet, and he felt as though he had the noblest job in the world. The quartermaster was tolerably complimentary to this RNVR "Snotty" (the naval term for a midshipman), who was amazed to learn that he had been steering *Hood* up the east coast for a full hour and a half, making 17 knots with three alterations of course.

The ship had two main passageways, one on the port side and one on the starboard. Newcomers to the ship could not tell whether they were going forward or aft, however, and it was only when a more experienced crewmember pointed out to Robin the small, telltale bulges on the supporting beams that carried the weight of the deck above that he could figure out where he was going.

Years later, in 1941, Board was serving on the destroyer *Garth,* which was on convoy duty off the north east coast. He was awakened in the middle watch and asked to decipher a signal for the captain, which had been sent out to the fleet. There were only two words: "*Hood* sunk." "It was dreadful," he says. "Nobody could believe it."

CHAPTER 7

Recollections
of an Engineer Artificer:
Hood's World Cruise

Engineer Artificer Frederick Bushell.

JOHN BUSHELL

FREDERICK REEVE BUSHELL WAS BORN IN SHERINGHAM, NORFOLK, in 1902. At age seventeen, he trained to be an engineer artificer (mechanic) on HMS *Fishguard* in Portsmouth Harbour. Shortly after completing his training, Bushell joined HMS *Hood,* which, as flag-ship of the British Special Service Squadron, was about to begin a world Cruise.

The world cruise was the idea of the commander in chief of the Atlantic Fleet, Sir John de Robeck, who saw it as a way of showing the flag and strengthening Britain's ties with her commonwealth. An earlier mission to Brazil had been a great success.

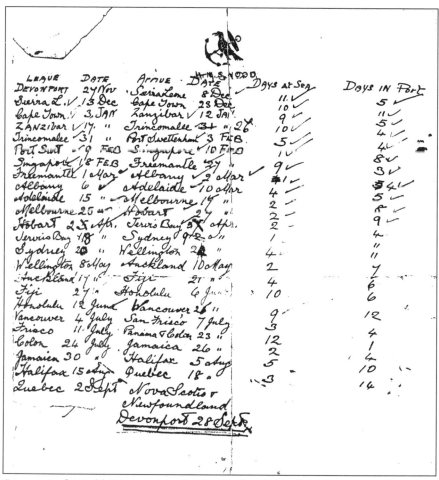

Itinerary of World Cruise, recorded by Frederick Bushell.

Hood embarked from Devonport at 7 A.M. on November 27, 1923, with Vice Adm. Sir Frederick L. "Tam" Field in command of the squadron. His flag captain and chief staff officer was John Im Thurn. They passed the Eddystone light at 8 A.M. and were joined by the battleship *Repulse,* commanded by Capt. Henry W. Parker, and the light cruisers *Delhi, Dauntless, Danae, Dragon,* and *Dunedin,* the last to be handed over to the New Zealand Navy.

At that time, HMS *Hood* carried a Fairey Flycatcher biplane, tiny by modern standards. The small platform on the top of B turret on

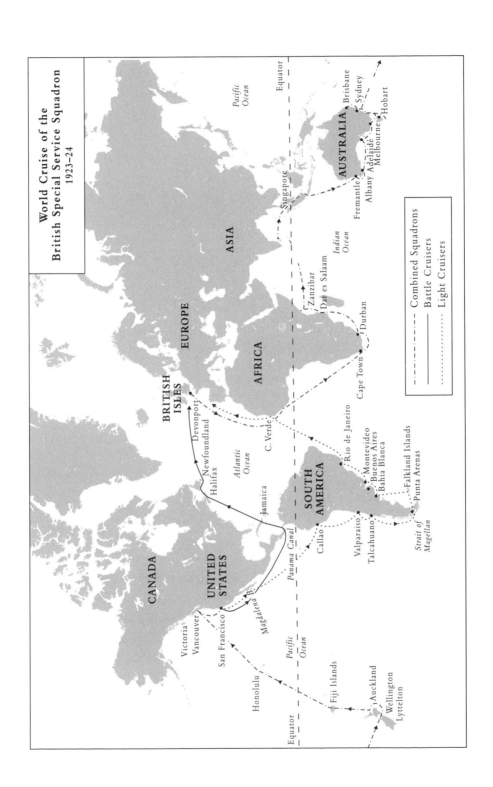

**World Cruise of the
British Special Service Squadron**
1923–24

Combined Squadrons — · — · —
Battle Cruisers ————
Light Cruisers ················

Pacific Ocean

Equator

ASIA

EUROPE

BRITISH ISLES

Devonport
Newfoundland
Halifax

Atlantic Ocean

C. Verde

AFRICA

Zanzibar
Dar es Salaam

Indian Ocean

Durban

Cape Town

Singapore

AUSTRALIA
Brisbane
Sydney
Hobart
Melbourne
Adelaide
Albany
Fremantle

Rio de Janeiro
Montevideo
Buenos Aires
Bahia Blanca
Falkland Islands
Punta Arenas

SOUTH AMERICA

Jamaica

Panama Canal

UNITED STATES

CANADA

Victoria
Vancouver

San Francisco

Magdalena B.

Callao
Valparaiso
Talcahuano

Strait of Magellan

Pacific Ocean

Honolulu

Fiji Islands

Auckland
Wellington
Lyttelton

Equator

which it was mounted could be rotated for takeoff. In normal circumstances, it would be flown only if the ship was in sight of land, as there were no facilities for it to land back onboard, or for its pilot to be recovered if it ditched in the sea. If it had to be flown in a battle situation far out at sea for reconnaissance or shell spotting, the pilot's chances of survival would be virtually zero.

Hood crossed the Bay of Biscay and passed Cape Finisterre about midday on November 29. As they steamed southward, Bushell noticed that the water became more phosphorescent, and as the ship cut through the ocean, it looked as though sparks were flying off the hull.

At 6:30 A.M. on December 3, amid great excitement, the coastline of Tenerife, one of the Canary Islands, came into view, and at noon the squadron stopped for a couple hours opposite Grand Canary Isle. Everyone was presented with a sun helmet and tropical gear. As they set sail again, the temperature below decks reached 105°. The crew marveled at how far the flying fish, which appeared in shoals, could glide over the water. In the afternoon, sharks were seen near the ship.

Bushell's duties included keeping watch and working to maintain the ship's boilers. During one of the watches, the temperature in boiler room A exceeded 140°. Three stokers collapsed with heat exhaustion, and the boilers had to be shut down. Two extra fans were provided for the mess, but the heat made staying below most uncomfortable.

On December 8, *Hood,* her paint fresh, her guns polished, and her company of Royal Marines on parade on deck, led the procession of ships into the harbor of Freetown, capital of Sierra Leone, where they dropped anchor. A flotilla of canoes arrived from shore, bearing local fruit. The sailors spent some time ashore, and then, on December 14 at 11 A.M., they set sail once more, maintaining a speed of 16 knots. The waters were alive with fish, including porpoises. The men held a ceremony when *Hood* crossed the equator on December 16, 1923.

Training ship HMS Fishguard. *Frederick Bushell standing, left.*

JOHN BUSHELL

They reached Cape Town on December 22, to find the top of Table Mountain covered with clouds. They were greeted by a crowd, some of whom had come from as far away as Pretoria just to see the fleet. At Cape Town, two of *Hood's* crew deserted.

Bushell was now mainly occupied with maintaining *Hood's* numerous boats, currently the admiral's barge, rather than working down below in the stifling hot boiler room. After leaving Cape Town, they avoided Port Elizabeth because of thick fog and anchored off East London, where they saw the first green scenery since leaving England. At Durban, the sailors swam in the warm waters of the Indian Ocean and met Zulu chiefs, who laid down their spears and shields before them in a gesture of goodwill. They made a visit inland to the town of Pietermaritzburg.

On January 12, *Hood* anchored off the island of Zanzibar, where she was dressed, and fired a Royal salute in honor of the sultan, Sayyad Khalifa ben Harud. Outrigger canoes came up and surrounded *Hood*.

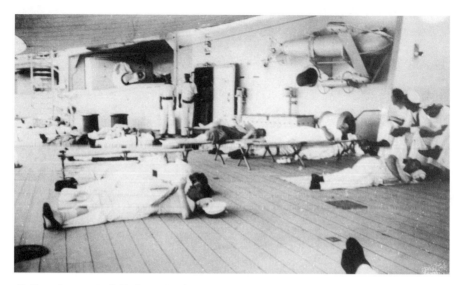

Sailors in tropical "whites" relaxing. FRED WHITE

Here were camels and palm trees, which many of *Hood*'s crew had never seen before, and a ruined fort with a collection of ancient muzzle-loading cannons. Bushell was amused to see a milepost that showed the exact distance from London.

It took nine days to complete the 3,000-mile journey to Ceylon, during which time they encountered torrential rain. Bushell, who slept on the upper deck, got soaked as he lay in his hammock. They took the opportunity to get in some gunnery practice, first using the 5.5-inch guns, with *Repulse* firing at *Hood*'s wake and *Hood* firing at hers, and later the 15-inch, with Bushell at his action station in the boiler room. On January 27, they reached Trincomalee, where, with its magnificent tropical gardens, the crew had its first rest in two months.

At Port Swettenham in Malaya, *Hood* had her first casualty when Able Seaman Lee succumbed to malaria. He was buried in the town cemetery. Here they saw splendid Chinese temples and a procession to celebrate the Chinese New Year. The men took a train trip to Kuala Lumpur, capital of the Federated Malay States.

Malaya—visit to a rubber estate. JOHN BUSHELL

Hood then set off for Singapore. On the way, there was a typhoon warning, and orders came down for all watertight hatches on the main deck to be closed, but the storm did not materialize. At Singapore, twenty-nine thousand people came to look over *Hood,* and it is said that Vice Admiral Field made so many speeches that his voice failed him.

Hood passed the island of Sumatra on February 15 and Christmas Island on the twentieth, when the men witnessed a lunar eclipse. The ship reached Freemantle, on the southwest coast of Australia, on the twenty-seventh, and here *Hood* was given a mascot, Joey the wallaby, with whom the crew members enjoyed playful boxing matches. Crowds of visitors packed the deck from morning until night, and Bushell's task was to inform them about *Hood*—her length and beam, how many boilers (twenty-four), how many screws (four), and so forth. The crew visited Perth and the Swan River, where the national sculling championships were held. When *Hood* was ready to leave, thousands came to watch the ship depart.

The journey to Adelaide was marred by heavy seas, which broke over the quarterdeck and caused the crockery to slide off the tables. *Hood* had to anchor seven miles offshore, as the harbor was too shallow, but nevertheless 18,510 visitors came to look over the great ship.

At Melbourne, where they stayed for eight days, this figure was greatly surpassed, with a total of 136,400 visitors coming aboard. So great was the crush that barricades were knocked down, women fainted, and children got lost. When some ladies invaded the restricted area to throw streamers, HMS *Delhi* held a competition to see who could throw one the highest. The crew made visits ashore, and the town hall was illuminated in their honor. The highlight of the visit came when the men of the British Special Service Squadron marched ceremonially through Bourke Street. At this point HMAS *Adelaide,* representing the Australian Navy, joined the world cruise.

After brief visits to Hobart in Tasmania and the Royal Australian Naval College at Jervis Bay on the continent's southwest coast, they arrived at Sydney on April 9. Everyone onboard—especially the "snotties," midshipmen who manned the picket boats and were responsible for ferrying visitors on and off the ship all day long and late into the night—was growing weary of the endless parties and social functions, and having to entertain visitors. However, the fifty-seven bags of mail from home that awaited them there did much to restore morale.

Hood encountered more rough weather on the voyage to Wellington, New Zealand, during which some lockers were washed away, as was the wallaby, which fortunately was able to keep afloat until rescued. Here the cruiser HMS *Dunedin* was handed over to the New Zealand Navy and *Hood* received a visit from Admiral Lord Jellicoe, hero of World War I, who was now New Zealand's governor general.

At Auckland, thousands lined the docksides. Lit up on the wall of the Harbour Board building were the words, *Haere Mai! Haere Mai!*, Maori for "Welcome! Welcome, gallant sons of the sea!"

The crew next spent six days at Suva, Fiji. Then, at Western Samoa, *Hood* and her companion ships were ringed with long canoes propelled by native oarsmen, twenty on each side.

Hood *at Freemantle.* JOHN BUSHELL

When the ships reached Honolulu, capital of Hawaii, thirty-two American seaplanes saluted the squadron by circling overhead as it entered Pearl Harbor. There the men visited sugar factories and pineapple plantations.

Having crossed the Pacific Ocean, the squadron arrived on June 21 at Vancouver, where the local people had tied totem poles to the lamp posts in welcome. Here *Hood's* soccer team was defeated by a team from the Royal Canadian Mounted Police.

After spending some time at San Francisco, the squadron split into two groups. *Hood, Repulse,* and *Adelaide* sailed eastward on a 3,442-mile journey to Panama, while the remaining four light cruisers continued down to Chile, the Falkland Islands, and Brazil, and eventually making their way home via Cape Verde in West Africa.

Hood reached the Panama Canal at 5 A.M. on July 23. The first lock she came to was the mile-long Miraflores. Here the ship was lifted in two stages, at the rate of six feet per minute, to a height of fifty-five feet above sea level. The six small but powerful electric trolleys, or "mules," that ran alongside the locks took *Hood* in tow, but

Hood *entering the first set of the three Gatun locks, Panama Canal.*

getting into the first lock was slow progress, as there was only about eighteen inches to spare on each side.

Hood, Repulse, and *Adelaide* then steamed through the Miraflores Lake and into the next lock, the Pedro Miguel, where they were raised another thirty feet. By 5 A.M. the next morning, they were in the eight-mile-long Calabra Cut, the highest point of which was 300 feet above sea level. From the artificial lake of Gatun, formed when the Valley of the Chagres was dammed, they entered the Gatun locks, which lowered them in three stages to the Atlantic Ocean, which, because of currents, tides, and winds is about eight inches lower than the Pacific. The cost of passing through the canal was $22,500.

After visiting Jamaica, on the Atlantic side, the ships headed north to the cold climes of Halifax, Nova Scotia, and from there to Quebec, which they reached on August 14. They journeyed down the St. Lawrence River to St. John's, Newfoundland, and then, at 4 P.M. on September 17, they weighed anchor and headed out into the Atlantic for the final leg of the journey.

At 3 P.M. on Sunday, September 28, the four light cruisers *Delhi, Dauntless, Danae,* and *Dragon* came into view off the Lizard peninsula and rejoined the squadron. The men had been away from home for ten months and a day, and for Bushell—though there were minor regrets, such as the never-ending problems with the boats, particularly the admiral's barge—it had been a wonderful trip. *Hood* had traveled a total of 38,153 miles, crossed the equator six times, received 752,049 visitors aboard, and entertained 37,770 at parties and dances. The number of visitors for the whole squadron was nearly 2 million.

PART TWO

·──◄█►──·

Death of a Ship

The German ~~pocket~~-battleship Bismarck *caught by photographic reconnaissance in Dobric Fjord.* HMSO

CHAPTER 8

The Stage Is Set

FLYING OFFICER SUCKLING PEERED THROUGH THE COCKPIT WINDOW of his Spitfire aircraft, not sure if he could believe his eyes. It was May 21, 1941, and he had been sent on a mission for the Photographic Reconnaissance Unit of RAF Coastal Command. The aircraft he was piloting had left Wick, on the northeast coast of Scotland, and flown as far as the Norwegian port of Bergen. It was near there, in the small Dobric Fjord, that he noticed two interesting shapes and identified them as warships, one large and one not so large, lying at anchor. It was then 1:15 P.M., and he was nearing the end of his search.

On returning to base, he made his report to the station intelligence officer, who examined the wet prints of the photographs Suckling had taken. The matter was reported to the headquarters of Coastal Command, where Air Marshal Sir Frederick Bowhill asked for the prints so that they could be further evaluated by his own staff.

The only aircraft available to transport them the 650 miles to London was Suckling's, so he was ordered to take off again and fly south. However, finding himself short of fuel, he put down on the outskirts of Nottingham, which was his hometown. From here, he and a friend journeyed at high speed in his friend's car, through the

Bismarck *leaving Bergen, May 1941, photographed from* Prinz Eugen.
R. N. MUSEUM

night and the blackout, and reached their destination in the small
hours of the morning. At Coastal Command's headquarters, the
Admiralty's photographic experts were able to identify the larger of
the two ships as the German pocket battleship *Bismarck* and the
smaller one as a heavy Hipper-class cruiser, later identified as *Prinz
Eugen,* which had evidently stopped to refuel.

Once the danger to Allied ships of magnetic mines had been
overcome by equipping them with degaussing equipment, the main
danger came from German U-boats hunting in packs and lurking on
the surface at night to attack convoys bringing vital supplies to
Britain from America and Canada. In the last six months of 1940,
285 ships totaling 1,470,388 tons were sunk in this way. The problem
was exacerbated by the fact that there were not enough destroyers to
provide the convoys with adequate escorts. Prime Minister Winston
Churchill turned for help to President Roosevelt, who made fifty
veteran American destroyers available for the purpose.

Also confronting the convoys was a new generation of German surface raiders, which, in October 1940, made their intentions clear when the German pocket battleship *Admiral Scheer* sailed from the German port of Brunsbuttel on the River Elbe, past Bergen and into the Norwegian Sea. She crossed the Arctic Circle, turned west, and on October 31 passed undetected by the British Admiralty through the Denmark Strait between Iceland and Greenland. She sank the solitary British ship the *Mopan* before it had time to send out a distress signal, and on November 5 she attacked the Halifax convoy, which was returning from Nova Scotia to England and was unaware of the German raider's presence. While the ships scattered in all directions and disguised their positions with smoke, the convoy's only escort, the armed merchant cruiser *Jervis Bay*, turned to confront the enemy. Though the odds were hopelessly against her, *Jervis Bay*'s courageous action enabled all but five of the thirty-seven merchant ships in the convoy to escape, and for his bravery, her captain, E. S. F. Fegen, was awarded a posthumous Victoria Cross.

In December 1940, the German heavy cruiser *Admiral Hipper* broke out through the Denmark Strait and, having attacked an Allied troop convoy, became the first German heavy warship to put into the French port of Brest.

Worse was to follow when, in January 1941, the battle cruisers *Scharnhorst* and *Gneisenau* evaded the British blockade and were taken by German admiral Gunter Lutjens through the Denmark Strait. In the course of two months, they sank a total of 116,000 tons of Allied shipping before turning for France.

The 49,000-ton *Bismarck* was named after Otto Eduard Leopold, Prince von Bismarck, who was chancellor of the German Empire from 1871 to 1890. With eight 15-inch guns, and capable of a maximum speed of 29 knots, she was launched on Valentine's Day, February 14, 1939, from the Hamburg shipyard of Blohm and Voss, at a state occasion in the presence of Adolf Hitler. On September 15, 1940, she sailed down the River Elbe for sea trials in Kiel Bay, and following further adjustments in Hamburg, she was ready by March 1941 to sail to the northern Polish port of Gdynia. Here she was joined by the newly built heavy cruiser *Prinz Eugen,* weighing 19,000 tons and capable of 32.5 knots, with an armament that included eight 8-inch guns and twelve torpedo tubes. She was named after the prince of Savoy, who had defended Vienna against the Turks in 1683. It was the intention of the German naval staff that these two ships be joined by *Scharnhorst* and *Gneisenau,* both currently in the French port of Brest, but this proved impossible, as the former could not be refitted in time and the latter had been damaged by a torpedo attack from an aircraft of Coastal Command.

It was the cruiser *Gotland,* from the neutral country of Sweden, that first sighted *Bismarck* and her escort *Prinz Eugen* in the Skagerrak Straits between Norway and Denmark on May 20, and by the following morning, this information had been passed to London. If these two ships managed to break out into the Atlantic, the consequences for Allied shipping would be unimaginable. Therefore, following Flying Officer Suckling's successful reconnaissance, the two German ships were attacked by six Whitley and six Lockheed Hudson bombers of Coastal Command, but the attack failed because of thick cloud cover.

It now became imperative to follow the movements of the two ships, and to this end, every available aircraft of Coastal Command on the east coast of Scotland and Yorkshire was pressed into service. However, the weather had closed in, and flying conditions were bad, with gales and clouds and dense haze extending down to sea level. On the afternoon of May 22, the commander of the Royal Naval Air Station at Hatston, Orkney, Capt. Henry St. J. Fancourt, was given permission from Coastal Command and from Adm. John Tovey, commander-in-chief of the Home Fleet, who was desperate for news, to fly a veteran American twin-engine Maryland bomber to reconnoiter the Bergen Fjords. He chose as pilot the experienced Lt. N. N. Goddard and as observer Commander G. A. Rotherham. In a magnificent feat of navigational and flying skills, they reached their destination, and at 7:39 that evening, Hatston Air Station was able to report to Admiral Tovey, "Following received from Hatston reconnaissance aircraft over Bergen. Battleship and cruiser have left."

All of this set in motion a sequence of events that would leave two of the world's finest capital ships lying at the bottom of the ocean and shake the foundations of the Royal Navy to its core.

Admiral Sir John C. Tovey,
Commander-in-Chief Home Fleet.
HMSO

Adm. Sir John Tovey studied the signal on his desk. He was now in possession of the news the entire Royal Navy had awaited. From the bridge of his flagship, *King George V,* he gazed out across the relatively safe waters of Scapa Flow, ten miles from the north coast of Scotland across the Pentland Firth and the traditional base of the Royal Navy. News that *Bismarck* and her heavy cruiser escort, later known to be *Prinz Eugen,* had been seen by the Swedish cruiser *Gotland* steaming through the Skaggerak passage between Norway and Denmark had first filtered through to the Admiralty in London and had now reached him on his flagship.

Tovey was aware that at this time, there were eleven convoys in the North Atlantic, six homeward and five outward bound, including the Troop Convoy WS 8B of five ships, which had left the Clyde on

May 22 bound for the Middle East, escorted by the cruisers *Exeter* and *Cairo* and eight destroyers. He also knew that there were five possible routes by which the two enemy ships first sighted by Flying Officer Suckling could break out into the North Atlantic.

An attempt through the Pentland Firth between Scotland and the Orkney Islands would be foolhardy, as it was well within the range of the air patrols and ships of the Home Fleet at their base at Scapa Flow. An attempt through the Fair Island Channel between the Shetlands and the Orkneys could also be discounted for the same reasons, unless the enemy took advantage of a spell of bad weather with poor visibility. The 160-mile-wide channel between the Shetlands and the Faroes was a possible option, as was the channel between the Faroes and the southeast coast of Iceland, which were separated by a distance of 250 miles. Most probable was the fifth option, through the Denmark Strait between Iceland and Greenland, an area notorious for fog. This route had previously been used successfully by the raiders *Admiral Scheer* and *Hipper* and successfully negotiated by the battleships *Scharnhorst* and *Gneisenau,* under Adm. Gunter Lutjens, who now commanded *Bismarck.* Although at this time of the year the Greenland icepack and the presence of a British minefield would leave the enemy with only about sixty miles of navigable waterway, the weather conditions were likely to be poor, making the British air and sea patrols less effective.

Accordingly, Tovey readied all ships in Scapa Flow to two hours' notice for steam, and when Flying Officer Suckling's mission had confirmed the presence of *Bismarck* and her Hipper-class cruiser escort in the fjord near Bergen, the three-funneled, 8-inch-gunned, county-class cruiser *Suffolk,* which was refueling at Hvalfjord in Iceland, was ordered to patrol in the Denmark Strait with her sister ship the cruiser *Norfolk.* Tovey had already ordered *Suffolk*'s captain R. M. Ellis on May 18 to watch this passage carefully, paying particular attention to the edge of the ice.

During the afternoon of May 21, the weather deteriorated, and in the absence of any further news, Admiral Tovey decided that he must remain at Scapa Flow but that in order to cover the northern approaches to the Atlantic, a battle cruiser fleet should set sail. This consisted of the battle cruiser HMS *Hood,* the newly commissioned battleship HMS *Prince of Wales,* and six destroyers, *Achates, Antelope, Anthony, Echo, Electra* and *Icarus. Hood* was now under the flag of Vice Adm. Lancelot E. Holland, who only ten days previously had relieved Vice Admiral Whitworth and was now second in command of the Home Fleet. She was commanded by Capt. Ralph Kerr. This force accordingly passed the Hoxa antisubmarine boom at 12:52 A.M. on May 22, the destroyers taking station ahead.

Admiral Tovey commanded his own flagship, *King George V,* and also the aircraft carrier *Victorious,* which, like *Prince of Wales,* had been commissioned only two months previously. Also at Tovey's disposal were the cruisers *Manchester* and *Birmingham,* with five trawlers, which were patroling the Iceland-Faroes channel; the cruiser *Arethusa,* which was being held in readiness at Reykjavik, Iceland; and the cruiser *Hermione,* which was on her way to join him at Scapa Flow.

On receipt of the signal from the Hatston Air Station that *Bismarck* and cruiser had left their moorings, Tovey ordered his ships to prepare for sea. *Arethusa* was ordered to join *Birmingham* and *Manchester,* and Vice Admiral Holland's battle cruiser force, instead of proceeding to Hvalfjord to fuel, and was ordered to cover the area to the southwest of Iceland. At 10:45 P.M. on May 22, Admiral Tovey, in *King George V,* with *Victorious,* the cruisers *Galatea, Hermione, Kenya,* and *Aurora,* and seven destroyers, left Scapa Flow. They were joined just before noon on May 23 by the veteran battle cruiser *Repulse,* which was coming up from the Clyde. This force would take up a central position ready to support the cruiser patrols on whichever side of Iceland the enemy might choose to come.

In addition, Admiral Tovey requested aerial reconnaissance of the Iceland-Faroes and Faroes–Shetland channels, the Denmark Strait, and the Norwegian coast. The weather was helping the enemy but was an increasing hindrance to Tovey, and at 6:30 A.M. on May 23, he received the signal "From Admiral, Rosyth: air reconnaissance postponed owing to weather." Air patrols of the Norwegian coast and the Denmark Strait had to be abandoned, as did the patrol of the Faroes-Shetland channel soon after noon. The Iceland-Faroes patrol was the only one that could be maintained throughout the day.

As the day wore on with no news of the enemy, the tension mounted for Admiral Tovey and his staff. He was aware that the poor weather conditions meant that there were many gaps through which the enemy might slip undiscovered, either by the cruiser patrols or by the few air patrols that could be flown. He also had to consider the possibility that the enemy might not be considering a breakout at all, but rather an invasion of Iceland or the Faroes. However, for the Allies, an attack on the Atlantic convoys would pose the greatest threat, and he therefore took immediate steps to counter it.

As *Hood, Prince of Wales,* and the destroyers of the battle cruiser force headed toward the southern approaches to the Denmark Strait, so Admiral Tovey's battle cruiser fleet struggled through increasingly heavy seas to cover the passages south of latitude 62°, so as to be in a position to intercept the enemy whatever tactic they should choose to employ.

Sgt. Thomas McLaren shifted uneasily in the seat of the Lockheed Hudson aircraft now taking off from Wick on the northeast coast of Scotland. His role on this trip was that of radio operator, but he would take over a gun position in an emergency. It was the morning of May 23, 1941. Also aboard the aircraft of RAF Coastal Command was the pilot, the second pilot-cum-navigator, who would take over in a case of emergency, and one air gunner. Their mission was to escort HMS *Hood, Prince of Wales* and their six destroyers.

They understood that *Hood*'s mission was to intercept the German pocket battleship *Bismarck* and the heavy cruiser *Prinz Eugen* and to prevent them from attacking the Allied convoys. The code letters "P.Q." meant that a convoy was en route from the United States to

Sergeant Thomas E. McLaren,
Wick, Scotland, 1941.

THOMAS McLAREN

the northern Russian ports of Archangel and Murmansk, and the code letters "Q.P." meant the reverse.

Takeoff from Wick was difficult. Drifting snow covered the ground, and the aircraft was weighed down with main tanks and overload tanks filled with fuel to enable it to remain airborne for approximately ten and a half hours. It also carried two depth charges of 250 pounds each and two 250-pound general-purpose bombs. The members of the crew were only too aware of their vulnerable situation.

Thomas McLaren, in his capacity as radio operator, observed a strict radio silence and kept a listening watch. One hour into the flight, the weather deteriorated still further, and the pilot had to decrease their altitude to avoid the danger of the wings icing up.

About two hours into the flight, they sighted the convoy, which immediately dispatched a destroyer to investigate this new arrival from the sky. The airmen were very cold in their flying suits and decided it was time for coffee. Even so, they felt happier to be in the air than on the sea, where the huge Atlantic waves were covering the ships below with spray, particularly *Hood,* which, with her lack of

Thomas McLaren's Hudson aircraft "T for Tommy" (nearest camera) of 220 Squadron RAF Coastal Command, Wick, searching for Bismarck *the day after the sinking of HMS* Hood. COURTESY OF THOMAS McLAREN

freeboard, was notorious as being a wet ship. McLaren knew that within a few hours he would be back at Wick in the sergeants' mess having a good meal, whereas the poor devils on the decks below were obliged to eat while remaining at their posts as the ships rolled from side to side.

Although McLaren thought *Hood* was the most impressive ship he had ever seen, the immense North Atlantic rollers made the huge ships seem small. Even the two capital ships looked like little more than matchsticks as they bounced around in the mighty sea. *Hood's* great length meant that she was always riding at least two waves at once, if not three. McLaren realized that if the ship went down in that water, her crew did not stand a chance.

The ships signaled to each other by flying flags stretched out on lines. Only naval personnel were taught to read these signals, but the young McLaren had made a special study of them and to the surprise of his fellow aircrew members, he could decipher the signals.

McLaren used the aircraft's lamp to signal both the destroyers and *Hood* the code letter of the hour. *Hood* acknowledged the signal and granted the aircraft permission to approach the convoy and to hold circuit at a three-mile radius. The crew kept a careful watch, particu-

Aerial view of Hood. *ROBIN BOARD*

larly of the rear quarters of the convoy, from which attacks from U-boats were most likely to take place.

Thirty minutes later, McLaren spotted some objects floating in the water directly in the path of the convoy. They discussed this over the intercom, and all agreed that these were probably mines, which could have broken loose in the previous day's storms—a mine would normally be tethered below the surface and therefore invisible. Or they may have been laid deliberately by an enemy U boat. McLaren was instructed to signal *Hood* and warn her of the danger. The signal was acknowledged and the convoy scattered. One destroyer set off to take care of the mines. The crew then settled down to normal circuits and observation.

McLaren then requested permission to close the aircraft's circuit to a mile, in order to take photographs. *Hood* requested that the aircraft change over to restricted-range wireless telegraphy, which had an approximate range of $6^{1}/_{2}$ miles, and then granted permission for the pilot to close in. He did, and took some excellent photographs.

By this time, with the visibility deteriorating, the wind strength increasing, and fuel getting low, the pilot decided to return to base. McLaren signaled to *Hood* again, wishing her and the convoy "God Speed and Good Hunting."

The aircraft arrived back at base at about 4 P.M. As McLaren made for the warmth of the mess, he thought grimly of his Royal Navy brothers riding out the vicious seas of the Atlantic. "Rather them than me," he thought, as he cradled a mug of steaming hot tea between his cold hands.

CHAPTER 9

The British Fleet

THE MIGHTY HOOD

Designed as a battle cruiser, HMS *Hood* was fast enough to chase and engage enemy cruisers, but sufficiently gunned to stand her ground and take on the slower but more heavily armored battleships. She truly was the "Mighty *Hood*," as she came to be known, and in a class of her own.

She was 40 feet longer than her opponent *Bismarck,* but 14 feet narrower in the beam. Both ships had eight 15-inch guns mounted in pairs. Her 12-inch-thick armored hull (or "belt") was flared at 12 degrees to the vertical to give her greater strength, with reinforced bulges below the waterline to protect against torpedoes.

Able Seaman Robert Ernest Tilburn, six feet tall and age twenty, had joined the ship's company four years previously in 1937. He had been with *Hood* at Oran when Admiral Somerville had been obliged to destroy the French Fleet when its commander, Admiral Gensoul, refused to scuttle his ships or sail them to a neutral port. Now his task was to man the port after 4-inch antiaircraft gun. Conditions on deck were appalling, and his waterproof cloth raincoat, or Burberry, was already beginning to go green with mold in the arctic cold and wet.

Hood's armor was not plate, but of the cemented type, with a high carbon content. Arranged in layers and with a surface made deliberately brittle, it was designed to be effective at breaking up enemy shells before they could penetrate deep into the ship's vitals. This protection consisted of a maximum of two inches thickness on the forecastle deck, two inches on the upper deck, two inches on the main deck, and three inches on the lower deck. Tilburn's action station on the 4-inch gun, however, was above the armor and therefore unprotected.

What Tilburn probably did not know was that though there had been plans to increase the thickness of *Hood*'s armored decks to give her extra protection from plunging shells as far back as 1938, because of the threat of war, this was never done. The job would have taken two years, and the British could not afford to have such a major ship out of service for so long.

Astern of Tilburn's gun position was the torpedo control tower and the quarterdeck, with its huge X and Y revolving 15-inch gun turrets, each with its own 30-foot rangefinder. Forward of him were the night defense and searchlight control positions, with each searchlight being rated at 120 million candlepower and designed for use in night action. Forward of this was the mainmast, with the engine room immediately below. Beneath him, deep down in the ship, was the 4-inch antiaircraft magazine, and each gun turret had a 15-inch magazine below it. *Hood* was unique in that, unlike in other ships, these latter magazines were situated above rather than below the shell-handling rooms.

Between the mainmast and the first of *Hood*'s two funnels was the boat deck, where were kept boats for every occasion. These included seven sailing boats: one 40-foot launch of double-diagonal construction, two 32-foot cutters, one 30-foot gig, two 27-foot whalers, and one 16-foot clinker-built dinghy. There were also three 35-foot fast motorboats, one serving as the admiral's barge; one 35-foot motor launch; and one 25-foot and one 16-foot motor dinghy. An antiquated 50-foot steam pinnace had previously been dispensed with.

Pom-pom gun crew, HMS Hood *October 1939.* ALICE E. REEKIE

Also on the boat deck, one on either side abreast of the boats, were situated two twenty-barreled unrotated projectile (UP) rocket mountings. These had been developed by the Air Ministry and adapted for use aboard ships and had come into service the previous year. A letter sent by Prime Minister Winston Churchill to Admiral Usborne in January 1940 described them as being of "immense importance." "The whole security of H.M. warships and merchant ships may be enhanced by this development." Sadly, this proved not to be the case. There were additional UP rocket mountings, one on either side of the forward funnel and a fifth on top of the forward B turret. Nine and a half tons of refill rockets were unsafely stored immediately below the launchers above the armor in splinter-proof lockers.

The UP rockets, which were a joke with the navy, were powered by solid fuel and designed to work in this way: When an enemy aircraft was observed approaching the ship, they were fired. On reaching a certain predetermined height, a small explosive charge separated the forward section from the rear propellant section. A parachute opened

Versatility of Hood's *guns.* FRED WHITE

15-inch ammunition. FRED WHITE

to suspend 400 feet of wire cable, at the end of which was a bomb. It was hoped that the aircraft would fly into the wire, whereupon the parachute would drag the wire along it until it impacted with the bomb. However, the rocket flight paths tended to be irregular, and they could be much affected by the wind. As far as is known, not one single loss was inflicted on the enemy by this method. In 1940, while *Hood* was at Gibraltar, a UP rocket accidentally went off. Its bomb exploded in the sea, but three of *Hood's* sailors suffered severe burns.

There were also on the boat deck large quantities of ready-use 4-inch and eight-barrel, 2-pounder pom-pom ammunition, also stored unsafely in thin steel lockers. This did not bode well for the ship if an enemy shell were to strike at this vulnerable point.

Hood's four 21-inch, above-water torpedo tubes, two on either side of the ship and protected by a mere $1^1/2$ inches of armor, were situated at the base of the mainmast only ninety feet from Tilburn's position. The warhead of each torpedo contained about 500 pounds of TNT, and the premature explosion of just one of these would be sufficient to break the ship in two.

Tilburn slapped his gloved hands together to keep warm. He glanced aft toward the stern and the receding barrels of the guns of X and Y turrets where, beyond the quarterdeck, was the great metallic sweep of the sea. He found himself wondering whether this was to be yet another wild goose chase. There had been more of them than he cared to remember. For months, *Hood,* from her base in Scapa Flow, had been engaged in a series of fruitless and abortive excursions. She had been sent to chase a German cruiser that was escorting a convoy off the Norwegian coast, but the operation was called off. She had been asked to cover the return of the cruisers *Berwick* and *Norfolk* and the aircraft carrier *Furious,* which had been sent to attack Tromso in Norway, but she had run into thick fog and had lost sight of her escorting destroyers. She had plowed through a gale and huge seas in an abortive attempt to locate a German cruiser and supply ships in the Iceland-Faroes gap. She had attempted unsuccessfully to locate and destroy *Admiral Scheer* after that ship's attack on the convoy, in which *Jervis Bay* was sunk. She had torn across the seas to the west of Ireland in search of Admiral Lutyen's ships *Scharnhorst* and *Gneisenau,* which had attacked the Halifax convoy and sunk 116,000 tons of Allied shipping, but the enemy had slipped through the net and made the safety of the French port of Brest. Finally, one month ago, on April 18, an erroneous message was received that *Bismarck,* two cruisers, and three destroyers had sailed from Kiel in a northwesterly direction, and *Hood,* with Adm. William Whitworth in command, the cruiser *Kenya,* and three destroyers were sent to patrol the northern waters. However, the operation was abandoned, and the force put into Hvalfjord, Iceland.

"Perhaps this time it will be different," Tilburn thought to himself. He hugged himself and rubbed his arms to keep warm, squinting as he peered out over the seas.

Royal Marine George Bradford Jackson, 1940. GEORGE JACKSON

HMS SUFFOLK

Marine George Bradford Jackson, aboard the county-class cruiser HMS *Suffolk,* hurried to assist the crew of X turret as they struggled to keep its twin guns operational.

Cruiser HMS Suffolk *at Scapa Flow.* GEORGE JACKSON

Jackson had first seen *Suffolk,* which had three funnels and eight 8-inch guns, as two tugs slowly pulled her into Scapa Flow. The stricken vessel had been hit by bombs off Stavanger, on the southern coast of Norway, and her stern and X turret were completely underwater. Those standing on the decks of the ships at Scapa Flow witnessed the event in shocked amazement. The detonation of the enemy shell had completely sealed off X turret, leaving no hope of survival for any of its occupants.

Since then, *Suffolk* had undergone a complete refit, which including having new Type 284 (range and direction-finding, or RDF) radar equipment, as well as Type 279 air-warning radar. Both were relatively recent innovations, and few ships had them at that time. The ship, which had been a virtual wreck, now seemed as good as new, but Jackson shortly discovered that that was not quite the case.

Jackson's job was to assist Petty Officer Woodfinden, the ordnance artificer of the now restored X turret, which was the Royal Marine turret. There were eight men, including the gunlayer and trainer, to work the twin 8-inch guns. Beneath was the shell room, with six

Suffolk *in the Denmark Strait.* GEORGE JACKSON

men, then the shell-handling room, with four men, and beneath this the magazine, with another four men. The magazine was sealed off, except for a door through which the cordite, the propellant charge for the shells, was pushed. Each cordite charge was about two feet long and six inches in diameter. It was white in color and enclosed in cotton mesh. No ferrous material was permitted, as it might cause a fatal spark. When the guns were fired, the noise inside the turret was bearable. Outside, however, it was a different matter.

So intense was the cold at this latitude that every hour the crew had to rotate the turrets and elevate and depress the guns to prevent them from seizing up. Because the repairs of the damage sustained at Stavanger were inadequate, the pipes of the hydraulic systems that worked the turrets were leaking, but somehow the men managed.

Suffolk had now been commissioned to go to the Denmark Strait, where she patrolled alone for about a week before she was joined by

Able Seaman Newell, lookout on HMS Suffolk, *who first sighted*
Bismarck *in the Denmark Strait.* R.N. MUSEUM

another ship of the First Cruiser Squadron, the *Norfolk,* also a
county-class cruiser, which had journeyed from Iceland. Like the
Suffolk, she also had three funnels and eight 8-inch guns.

While Jackson was effectively sealed up in his gun turret, lookout
Able Seaman Newell of the Red Watch scanned the horizon off *Suffolk's* starboard quarter and marveled at how the ice bank, glowing
pink beneath the setting sun, contrasted with the gun-metal gray of
the sea. Suddenly he saw a sight he would never forget. "Ship bearing green one-four-oh degrees!" he cried, and as the captain and
officers rushed to the side of the bridge, the cry became "Two ships
bearing green one-four-oh!" There, before their eyes, were the terri-
fying black hulks first of *Bismarck* and then of *Prinz Eugen,* bearing
toward them out of the mist at 28 knots. It was 7:22 P.M. on Friday,
May 23.

"Hard aport!" shouted Captain Ellis, the commanding officer of
Suffolk, and as his ship glided into the safety of the mist, he sighed

with relief that the enemy apparently had not spotted them. *Suffolk* immediately sent out an enemy report by wireless telegraphy: "One battleship, one cruiser in sight bearing 020 degrees distant 7 miles." The enemy ships were steering southwestward and skirting the edge of the ice.

Jackson tensed as he heard Captain Ellis announce that two ships had been picked up on the RDF and *Suffolk*, which prior to that had been "closed up in case anything happened" (with doors, hatches, and ventilation valves closed in order to limit damage), then promptly went to full action stations. As he manned the pump, trying desperately to keep the leaking water (a result of an earlier hit while in action at Stavanger in Norway) from flooding the gun turret, the huge white battle flag, with its red cross of St. George and the Union Jack in the top corner, was hoisted to fly proudly from the mainmast.

Suffolk was no match for a battleship, so she kept her distance, about fifteen miles, but some of the enemy's shells could travel more than twenty miles. All they could do, Jackson said, "was to keep silent, keep watch, and keep tracking." The radar made this possible in the thick mist. In fact, they wound up tracking the enemy for a total distance of 1,750 miles.

The ship was closed up for action, with everything battened down and all watertight doors closed and sealed. If a door was left open or its cleats were not properly locked, an explosion could cause it to fly open, permitting flash, blast, and heat to penetrate to the ship's vitals. Therefore, those in the magazines had to be shut off. They had no communication with the outside at all, apart from the intercom, and could get out only if they were let out.

From his position in the turret, Jackson could hear only the sounds of the ship's propellers, which were driving her along at a speed of 30 knots, faster than cruisers ordinarily travel. So tightly were Jackson and his shipmates sealed in that even if the forward A and B turrets fired their guns, neither he nor any of his turret's occupants would have been aware of it.

There followed a game of cat and mouse. The enemy, who also had radar, was now aware of the presence of the British cruisers and made continual changes in course to try to shake them off, even at one point making a complete 180-degree turn in order to confront them. Meanwhile, the cruisers hung on grimly, shadowing the enemy with their RDF and trying to keep them on the starboard bow with the light behind. Occasionally the watchers on *Suffolk* would see a burst of smoke as they attempted to keep visual contact at the comparatively safe distance of nine to fifteen miles. When they lost sight, they switched on the RDF again and resumed sweeping "Red 90 to Green 30."

The cruisers received a signal saying that a British Sunderland aircraft was on its way, and shortly afterward the watchers saw flashes of gunfire dead ahead and assumed this was the enemy firing at it. At 10:59 P.M., the enemy ships changed position so *Prinz Eugen* was now in front. At six minutes past midnight on May 24, when the visibility had dropped to a mere three-quarters of a mile, *Suffolk* sent out an enemy report: "Enemy hidden in snowstorm." They had lost contact. It was what everyone had feared.

As she threaded her way between chunks of floating ice, *Suffolk* was now having difficulty in maintaining wireless telegraphy contact with both Scapa Flow and *Norfolk*. But at 2:52 A.M., *Norfolk* signaled, "Large unknown vessel bearing 298 degrees." At 2:56 A.M., *Suffolk* was back in RDF contact at a range of nine miles.

HMS *NORFOLK*

While fifty-three-year-old William Frederic Wake-Walker was rear admiral aboard the cruiser HMS *Norfolk*, his younger son, Cedric, was aboard *Suffolk*, working in the transmitting station down in the bowels of the ship, and his elder son, Christopher, was aboard the cruiser HMS *Sheffield*, part of Admiral Somerville's Force H sailing northward from Gibraltar to reinforce. When *Bismarck* finally met her end, all three of these ships would be in on the kill.

*Admiral Sir William Frederic
Wake-Walker KCB, CBE.*

LADY ANNE WAKE-WAKER

Rear Admiral Wake-Walker glanced over the charts being scruti-
nized by his navigating officer. His flagship HMS *Norfolk* had now
joined Capt. R. M. Ellis's *Suffolk* in the Denmark Strait.

It was May 23 and at this time of year, the width of the Denmark
Strait between the Greenland ice edge and the Icelandic coast was
roughly sixty miles. As *Suffolk* patrolled between the ice and the
minefield the British had laid to the northwest of Iceland, the visibility was relatively good over the water to about ten miles. However,
the area where *Norfolk* patrolled, a dozen or so miles to the south,
had a lot of mist and fog. *Suffolk* was in a slightly more advantageous
position to shadow the enemy than *Norfolk,* because she had a
sophisticated type of radar that could cover all angles of bearing, with
the exception of the stern, whereas *Norfolk* was fitted with an unro-
tatable gunnery radar that could cover only a limited arc directly
ahead of the vessel.

The rear admiral was aware that it was not the practice of the
enemy's capital ships to engage with British warships. Instead, they

would evade them and concentrate solely on getting out into the Atlantic to create havoc with the vital shipping convoys. The role of his cruisers, therefore, was not to engage an enemy with the superior firepower of a battleship such as *Bismarck,* but to shadow the enemy with the object of guiding the British capital ships into their path. Nevertheless, if the enemy were suddenly to appear out of the mist, he knew that his ship would probably face extinction before he and his ship's company had even heard the scream of a 15-inch shell.

On receipt of *Suffolk's* signal that she had sighted the enemy, *Norfolk's* captain A. J. L. Phillips altered course with the object of getting into a shadowing position astern, by which time *Suffolk* had maneuvered to allow the enemy to pass her by. *Norfolk* then took up her position on the enemy's port quarter. In order to keep up, both ships were obliged to travel at almost their maximum speed of 29 knots.

Suddenly, at 8:30 P.M., the worst happened, when *Norfolk* emerged from the mist to find *Bismarck* and *Prinz Eugen* a mere six miles away on the port bow, and on a virtually reciprocal course. With the range decreasing rapidly, Captain Phillips ordered, "Hard astarboard," and as his ship made smoke, *Bismarck* opened fire. Columns of water shot up into the air as three out of five salvos of 15-inch shells straddled *Norfolk* before she reached the safety of the mist. Even here the rear admiral could not be certain he was safe and not being tracked by *Bismarck's* radar. The first shots of the Battle of the Denmark Strait had been fired.

Two minutes later, at 8:32 P.M., *Norfolk* made her first enemy report: "One battleship and one cruiser in sight . . ." It was good that she did so, because although *Suffolk* had been the first to sight the enemy, none of the enemy reports had gotten through, as the ship's aerials had iced up. It was therefore only this invaluable sighting report by *Norfolk* that gave Admiral Tovey, the commander in chief, his first confirmation of the presence of the enemy in the Denmark Strait.

The cruisers maintained their radar surveillance of the enemy at a range of about twelve miles and were able to make the occasional visual sighting through gaps in the snow, rain, and mist. There was always the danger that the enemy, now aware of their presence, might make a sudden about-turn and confront them, which, in fact, they did on one occasion but without success. The lookouts on the British ships were sometimes fooled by the presence of mirages into thinking that the enemy was bearing down upon them.

Because of Vice Admiral Holland's enforced radio silence, it was only at 4:45 A.M. on May 24, when a report was intercepted from *Icarus*, one of the destroyers with *Hood*, that Rear Admiral Wake-Walker became aware of the presence of the battle cruiser fleet in the vicinity, which was now closing in at high speed.

Then, at 5:48 A.M., almost ten and a half hours after she had first sighted the enemy ships, *Suffolk* received a signal from Vice Admiral Holland in the flagship *Hood*: "From *Hood*. 1 Battleship and 1 Cruiser bearing 337 degrees, 17 miles." The first objective had been achieved.

As the battle commenced, *Suffolk* reported that the weather was almost perfect, the visibility clear, the sun shining, only a few clouds in the sky, the wind not appreciable, but the temperature icy.

HMS *PRINCE OF WALES*

Astern of *Hood* and on her starboard quarter steamed the battleship HMS *Prince of Wales*. The two ships had been practicing signaling ever since leaving Scapa Flow. Sister ship of Admiral Tovey's flagship HMS *King George V, Prince* was built in Cammell Laird's shipyard at Birkenhead. Damaged in the enemy bombing of Liverpool, she was completed two months behind schedule, only as recently as January 19, 1941.

She had a displacement of 43,786 tons and was 745 feet long, with a beam of 103 feet. Her armament included ten 14-inch guns, six forward and four aft (in two four-gunned turrets and one two-gunned), and three UP rocket projectors. She was fitted with Type 279B air-warning radar and, like *Hood,* Type 284 main armament

Captain J. C. Leach DSO,
MVO, RN. ADMIRAL OF
THE FLEET SIR HENRY LEACH

Battleship HMS Prince of Wales, *from Gibraltar Chronicle,*
December 11, 1941. CDR. G. A. G. BROOKE

gunnery radar. She also carried two aircraft. Her captain, forty-seven-year-old John Catterall Leach, was a close friend of Admiral Tovey, despite the difference in rank.

Prince of Wales had only recently left the dockyard and joined the fleet a mere seven weeks before. There had been problems with her guns, and some civilian dockyard engineers had to sail with her. The main problem was that in the effort to make her magazines secure against shell flash, there was insufficient clearance and therefore a propensity for the quadruple turrets in particular to jam. There also had been insufficient time for her crew to complete their gunnery trials.

Admiral Tovey debated whether to signal to Vice Admiral Holland that *Prince,* whose armor he considered to be superior to *Hood's,* though that was debatable, should be stationed ahead of *Hood,* leaving the latter to stand off and fire from long range. He decided against it, however, saying, "I did not feel such interference with so senior an officer justified."

CHAPTER 10

Into Battle

Vice-Admiral Lancelot Holland CB.

TED BRIGGS

VICE ADMIRAL HOLLAND, ABOARD HIS FLAGSHIP, HMS *HOOD,* STIFF-ened as he read the signal received at 8:04 P.M. on the evening of May 23. The enemy report from the cruiser *Suffolk* informed him that *Bismarck* and her heavy cruiser escort had been sighted in the Denmark Strait. His commander-in-chief, Admiral Tovey, would not receive this news for another twenty-eight minutes, and then from the cruiser *Norfolk.*

This information put the enemy 300 miles and 005°, or virtually due north of the battle cruiser fleet. At 8:54 P.M., Holland turned west to 295° and increased speed to 27 knots to intercept.

Second in command of the Home Fleet under Admiral Tovey, and in command of HMS *Hood,* Lancelot Ernest Holland had taken over from Vice Admiral Whitworth only as recently as May 11. Age fifty-four, he was small and slim, and of a quiet, unperturbable disposition. He wore his hair, which was white, parted an inch left of center. He stood attired in a greatcoat and sea boots, with binoculars slung around his neck. Holland's naval pedigree was impressive and his promotion meteoric. Before taking command of *Hood,* he had commanded a cruiser squadron in the Mediterranean. His knowledge of gunnery and naval tactics was probably second to none. He was lacking in battle experience, however, and the nearest he had come to a major encounter was during the previous autumn, when, on Adm. James Somerville's orders, he had taken five cruisers to attack the Italian battle fleet off Cape Spartivento in Calabria, on the toe of Italy. The enemy chose not to engage his forces and made their escape.

Now, instead of conducting the operation in the traditional way, from the admiral's bridge, Holland decided to occupy the compass platform, situated high up in the control tower 110 feet above sea level and 90 feet above the deck. Also present were Flag Captain Kerr; Lieutenant Commander Wyldbore-Smith; Commander Gregson, the squadron gunnery officer; Lieutenant Commander Owens, the admiral's secretary; Commander Warrand, the squadron navigating officer; eighteen-year-old Bill Dundas, the action midshipman of the watch; Chief Yeoman Carne, who was attending the captain; Yeoman Wright, who looked after the demands of the officer of the watch at the binnacle (compass); and eighteen-year-old Ted Briggs, who was signalman.

In view of the probability of action, the ship's company was warned to change into clean underwear, the rationale being that if they were unfortunate enough to be wounded, the wound would be less likely to turn septic. Otherwise, the standard attire was number three suit, duffle coat, waterproof coat (Burberry), life belt, and steel helmet. The men wore antiflash gear—white gloves and white hoods—to protect their hands and heads from burns, and gas masks slung in front of their chests.

Hood's destroyers were ordered to follow at best speed in the moderate swell, and for a time they were unable to keep up and dropped away astern. They eventually regained contact, and at 11:18 P.M., they were ordered to go on ahead and form a screen. At midnight, reports put the enemy 120 miles distant at 010° and steering approximately 200°. By that time, *Hood* had altered course slightly to 285° at 27 knots.

Holland's plan of action had already been signaled by him to Captain Leach in *Prince of Wales.* The two ships were to advance in close order, with *Prince* stationed at four cables' lengths, or 800 yards, on *Hood's* starboard quarter. They would be maneuvered as a single unit, in accordance with the Admiralty's current fighting instructions, as drawn up in 1939 by Admiral of the Fleet Sir Dudley Pound.

In order to keep the target area they presented to a minimum, they would attack end-on, with their bows pointing straight toward the enemy. *Hood* and *Prince of Wales* would concentrate their fire on *Bismarck* while the cruisers *Norfolk* and *Suffolk* attacked *Prinz Eugen.* They were to observe radio silence at all times, and the use of radar was forbidden unless action was imminent, the object being to achieve the crucial element of surprise, which would be lost if the enemy were to pick up a signal from either ship. Although *Prince of Wales* was apprised of Holland's intentions, the maintenance of radio silence meant that Admiral Wake-Walker, in command of *Norfolk* and *Suffolk,* was kept in ignorance. Whether it was an oversight on Holland's part to employ neither the cruisers nor the destroyers in the forthcoming fray, or whether he considered the two capital ships to be strong enough in their own right to go it alone, will never be known.

It was now May 24, 1941, Empire Day. At eight minutes past midnight, Holland had the speed reduced to 25 knots and the course altered to due north. By making this 75-degree turn to starboard, Holland indicated that he was anxious to close with the enemy as

Hood *at speed.* JOHN WILLIAMS

quickly as possible. His aim likely was to corner the enemy ships while they were still confined to the southern narrows of the Denmark Strait, with the great ice bank to the west, and before they could elude him and gain the freedom of the wide reaches of the North Atlantic Ocean. He was also perhaps mindful of the weather conditions.

In May, the arctic twilight lasts virtually all night long, and although there is a five-hour period of comparative darkness, the sun is just below the horizon. Had Holland maintained his former course and speed, he could have expected to intercept the enemy at approximately 2:30 A.M., which would have meant going into action in the darkest period of the night. By turning north, he would bring the action forward and, provided he was correct in assuming that his battle cruiser fleet and the enemy were now on reciprocal courses and closing at a combined rate of about 60 knots, it was anticipated that contact would be made shortly after 1:40 A.M. Holland knew that the sun would set at 1:51 A.M., when, all being well, his targets would be nicely silhouetted against its afterglow.

At 12:15, final preparations were made. Battle ensigns were hoisted, and great white flags, some of the largest in the navy, at twenty-four feet long and twelve feet wide, fluttered from the yardarms of *Hood* and *Prince*. Almost as soon as this was done, the cruisers reported that they had lost touch with the enemy, who had run into a snowstorm.

Holland faced a dilemma. Below decks, in the two British capital ships, nearly three thousand men were closed up at action stations, but now the initiative, which had been his, had been snatched away. At 12:31, he signaled to *Prince of Wales* that if the enemy was not in sight by 2:10 A.M., he would probably alter course to 180°, due south, until the cruisers regained touch. This was to avoid the possibility that the enemy would outflank its pursuers. Holland hoped to use *Prince's* Walrus seaplane, but because of the poor visibility, it could not be catapulted off and was therefore defueled and stowed away. Holland did not try to use his ship's radar, which would have been useless anyway, as the enemy was too far to the north and therefore out of range.

At 2:03 A.M., with no further sightings from the cruisers, Holland altered course to 200° and permitted the crews of his two capital ships, who had been at their posts for more than four hours, to go to relaxed action stations. The destroyers, meanwhile, were ordered to continue the search northward. The question now was whether the enemy had made a change of course.

At 2:47 A.M., *Suffolk* regained contact with the enemy, and by 3 A.M., almost three hours after her last signal, reports began to come in again. To Holland's immense relief, the enemy had neither doubled back nor sunk the shadowing cruisers, but had continued on a southsouthwesterly course. However, Holland had now lost so much bearing on *Bismarck* and her consort that his proposed end-on approach was impossible. At 3:53 A.M., *Hood* increased speed to 28 knots, and at 4 A.M., the enemy was estimated to be twenty miles to the northeast.

By 4:30 A.M., visibility had increased to twelve miles, and at 4:40 A.M., *Prince* was ordered once again to prepare her Walrus seaplane for use. But water had penetrated its fuel tank, and it could not be made ready before the action commenced. The extra shell-spotting capability that the aircraft would have given Holland was now lost to him. Meanwhile, the gap was narrowing.

Many of the crews had spent all night at their posts, and the lookouts, enshrouded in their Burberrys, were passed steaming cups of cocoa to keep out the cold. At 5:10 A.M., as day was dawning, Holland gave the signal "Prepare for instant action!" Meanwhile, Captain Leach told his ship's company that they could expect to be in action within fifteen minutes, and his chaplain broadcast Sir Jacob Astley's prayer, said before the battle of Edgehill in 1642: "O Lord! thou knowest how busy I must this today: if I forget thee, do not thou forget me."

The captains, officers, and lookouts of the two great ships kept their binoculars trained on the horizon as they began to slowly emerge from the shadows of the night. The mighty *Hood* had hosted many a children's party in her time, both in home ports and throughout the world, and happy laughter had reverberated through the ship. Now the atmosphere was one of concentration and expectancy, tinged with fear.

Suddenly, at 5:35 A.M., word came by voice-pipe from the spotting position high above the compass platform: "Alarm starboard green 40!" At 5:37 A.M., *Prince of Wales* reported, "Enemy in sight distant 17 miles." *Bismarck* was bearing 330°, and *Prinz Eugen* appeared to be behind her.

Captain Ralph Kerr CBE, RN by Oswald Birley. JANE HAY

As soon as the enemy was sighted, Capt. Ralph Kerr of *Hood* ordered his pilot to make the enemy report: "Emergency to Admiralty and C-in-C., Home Fleet. From BC1 [battle cruiser 1]—one battleship and one heavy cruiser, bearing 330, distance 17 miles. My position 63-20 north, 31-50 west. My course 240. Speed 28 knots." Kerr knew only too well that Admiral Tovey and his main battle fleet were 300 miles away—or ten hours steaming—and therefore there was no

Forward turrets and control tower. FRED WHITE

possibility whatsoever of Tovey being able to reach them in time for the forthcoming action. The battle cruiser fleet was on its own.

Kerr had joined *Hood* as successor to Captain Glennie on February 15, 1941. Quiet and unobtrusive, he was easily recognizable by the large birthmark on his face. The navy was his life. There was no time for anything else. The following month, while *Hood* was undergoing a refit at Rosyth, on the River Forth, he had been present for the visits of King George VI and Queen Elizabeth and Winston Churchill. A destroyer man at heart, he is alleged to have told a colleague, "Let's get rid of the flat-irons [capital ships] and, having got them out of the way, the destroyers can have a proper war."

At 5:37 A.M., Vice Admiral Holland ordered the flag deck to hoist flag "Blue 4," and *Hood,* with *Prince of Wales* on her starboard quarter, duly turned together 40° to starboard toward the enemy. The two squadrons had previously been sailing on almost parallel courses, and his intention now was to close the range as rapidly as possible.

A 15-inch Shoot. FRED WHITE

Twelve minutes later, Holland ordered a turn of another 20° to starboard, putting *Hood* and *Prince of Wales* on a course of 300°, and gave the order to concentrate fire on the left-hand enemy ship, which he believed was *Bismarck* but which was in fact *Prinz Eugen.* This mistake arose because the silhouettes of the two enemy ships were virtually identical. Holland quickly realized his error and ordered, "Shift target right," but valuable seconds had been lost. Lt. Comdr. Colin McMullen, the gunnery control officer on *Prince of Wales,* however, had identified the two enemy ships correctly and already had his guns trained on *Bismarck.*

This extra turn toward the enemy closed the "A arcs"—in other words, it prevented the after turrets of the two British ships for the time being from being brought to bear. Therefore, only four of *Hood's* eight 15-inch and six of *Prince's* ten 14-inch guns were in action. *Prince* was further handicapped in that one of her forward guns was capable of firing only a single round because of a defect in the loading mechanism, which had been known beforehand. *Bismarck,* on her course, however, was able to bring all eight of her 15-inch guns to bear and fire broadside.

The hydraulic apparatus that worked the turrets grunted and hissed and the rangefinders swiveled as the guns of the forward A and B turrets lifted. Then Holland gave the order "Open fire!" and Chief Yeoman Carne shouted to the flag deck, "Flag 5, hoist!" It was 5:52 A.M., and the range was now down to 26,500 yards, or 15 miles, a position favorable to the British ships, which were becoming progressively less vulnerable to the plunging 15-inch shell fire.

Captain Kerr then ordered, "Open fire!" and the gunnery control officer shouted, "Shoot!" The *ting-ting* of the fire gong echoed through the loudspeaker at the rear of the bridge, and an ear-splitting roar announced *Hood's* first 15-inch salvo. A few seconds later, a 14-inch salvo followed from *Prince Of Wales.* Both ships concentrated on *Bismarck.*

The accuracy of a ship's gunnery was dependent largely on two factors: estimation of range and estimation of bearing. Both British and German ships were equipped with optical rangefinders, their accuracy being in direct proportion to their base length—the longer the rangefinder, the more accurate it was. *Hood* had one 30-foot rangefinder mounted on each of her four 15-inch gun turrets, another on the armored conning tower forward of the main control tower, a smaller, 9-foot one above the compass platform, and a 9-foot one high above it on the spotting top. Another 15-foot rangefinder on the spotting top had been removed when *Hood's* Type 284 gunnery radar was fitted. Holland was to rue the absence of this rangefinder later.

Hood also had several director firing sights, instruments designed to give an accurate bearing of an enemy ship, and consisting of a turntable fitted with telescopes, handwheels, and three seats. The gun trainer's task was to keep the enemy in his sights by moving the

Hood's forward turrets engulfed by spray. FRED WHITE

director and turret in a horizontal plane. *Hood's* main director was situated in the conning tower, and another was sited high up on the spotting top. In addition, each of the 15-inch gun turrets also had its own director in case local control should be required, as did the smaller secondary armament, right down to the pom-pom guns. The torpedo control tower was also equipped with a director.

Instead of each turret acting independently, information gleaned from the rangefinders and directors was telephoned to the director-layer in his gunnery control position. He made sure that the guns were elevated correctly, and adjusted the bearing according to the course and speed of his ship and that of the enemy. He also had to take into account other factors, such as air density and wind conditions, and lookouts high up on the spotting top observed the fall of shot and reported it back to him.

When the director-layer received orders from the bridge to fire, he pressed the trigger of his firing pistol, and every gun on the ship that was ready fired. This method was designed to eliminate the errors that could occur when a gunlayer in an individual turret had his work disrupted by smoke, spray, and splinters caused by enemy shell fire.

With salvo firing, each gun was aimed slightly differently so that the shells would fall in a pattern, with a spread similar to that of a shotgun. A straddle was achieved when splashes appeared simultaneously on either side of the target, and the fire controller could then achieve hits by reducing the spread of his salvo.

Hood's gunnery was probably second to none in the navy, but with one possible flaw being that when she was steaming at speed, her lowness in the water meant that her optical rangefinders were likely to be obscured by spray.

As battle was joined, Captain Kerr had no reason to be pessimistic. Although the A arcs of the two British ships were closed, they had an advantage of nine heavy guns to *Bismarck*'s eight, and they presented a far smaller target than she did by virtue of their angle of approach.

CHAPTER 11

Hood Goes Down

Ted Briggs on way to join Hood
from HMS Ganges, June 1939.

TED BRIGGS

YOUNG TED BRIGGS STOOD PROUDLY AT HIS STATION. HE HAD
joined *Hood* as signal boy on March 7, 1938, a week after his fif-
teenth birthday, having spent sixteen months training at HMS *Ganges*
near Ipswich. The outbreak of war was only thirty-six days away.

During his time on *Hood,* he had witnessed the destruction of the
French fleet at Mers-el-Kebir, in which she had played a part; been
aboard when she was bombed by the Italian Air Force in the
Mediterranean; and participated in numerous attempts to protect
convoys and keep German warships out of North Atlantic waters.
Now, three years later, he had advanced to ordinary signalman and
was stationed on *Hood*'s compass platform, manning the voice-pipe to
the flag deck, where his friends Ron Bell and Frank Tuxworth, and

Yeoman Bill Nevett, who was in charge, were ready to run up their vice admiral's signals. His other duties included collecting messages for the flag lieutenant and taking them to his cabin. As signalman, also, he had to know how to send messages in Morse code using a masthead flashing light. He was aware that Vice Admiral Holland had finally permitted *Hood*'s radar to be turned on and that *Bismarck* had been identified at a distance of twenty miles.

As *Hood*'s guns roared, he counted the seconds—up to twenty-five—until water spouts appeared close to the two dots that were the enemy ships on the horizon. Then, from the spotting position, came a voice: "We're shooting at the wrong ship! *Bismarck*'s on the right, not the left!"

Hood and *Prince of Wales* were steaming at 28 knots into increasingly heavy seas and a strengthening wind and, as feared, spray was obscuring their forward optical rangefinders. This meant that they were forced to open fire based on information provided by the smaller, and therefore less accurate, rangefinders situated in their control towers. The enemy, however, had the advantage of the "weather gauge" (a position on the windward side of the opponent). This meant that when they opened fire broadside at the British ships that were on their beam, they would be under no such constraints.

Over the next two minutes, *Hood*'s forward turrets fired six salvos each at *Bismarck* without reply. Holland had achieved the element of surprise. Briggs thought that the third had probably hit, because it sparked off a small glow. Then four starlike flashes, red in the center, appeared along *Bismarck*'s side, followed by a sound like a linen sheet being torn in half, as four 15-inch shells passed overhead. *Bismarck*'s second salvo fell into the water near *Hood*'s starboard beam, sending up four dirty brown water spouts. *Hood*'s crew members were all thrown off their feet. Commander "Tiny" Gregson, the gunnery officer, walked out onto the starboard wing of the compass platform and reported to Holland, "We've been hit at the base of the mainmast, sir, and we're on fire."

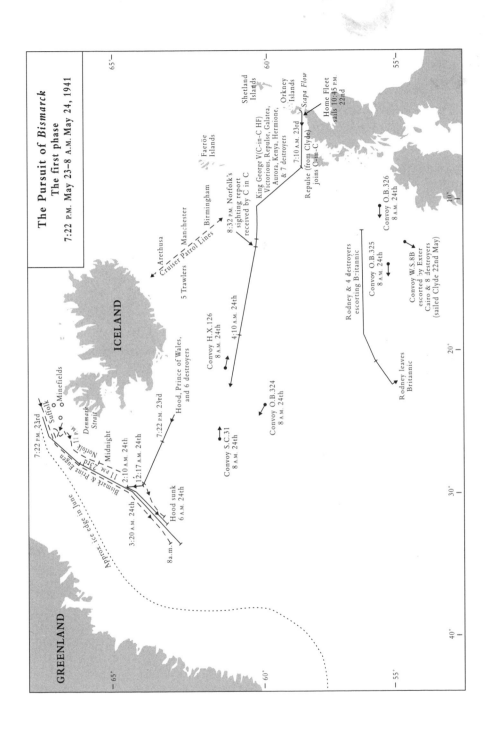

The Pursuit of *Bismarck*
The first phase
7:22 P.M. May 23–8 A.M. May 24, 1941

GREENLAND

ICELAND

Approx. ice edge in June

7:22 P.M. 23rd
Suffolk
Minefields
Denmark Strait
11 P.M.
Norfolk
Bismarck & Prinz Eugen
Midnight
11 P.M. 23rd
2:10 A.M. 24th
12:17 A.M. 24th
Hood sunk 6 A.M. 24th
3:20 A.M. 24th
8 a.m.
7:22 P.M. 23rd
Hood, Prince of Wales, and 6 destroyers

CN Arethusa
Cruiser Patrol Lines
5 Trawlers Manchester
Birmingham

Convoy S.C.31
8 A.M. 24th
Convoy O.B.324
8 A.M. 24th
Convoy H.X.126
8 A.M. 24th
4:10 A.M. 24th

Faeröe Islands

8:32 P.M. Norfolk's sighting report received by C in C

King George V (C-in-C HF)
Victorious, Repulse, Galatea,
Aurora, Kenya, Hermione,
& 7 destroyers

7:10 A.M. 23rd
Repulse (from Clyde)
joins C-in-C

Shetland Islands

Orkney Islands
Scapa Flow
Home Fleet sails 10:45 P.M. 22nd

Rodney & 4 destroyers
escorting B-itannic

Convoy O.B.325
8 A.M. 24th

Rodney leaves Britannic

Convoy O.B.326
8 A.M. 24th

Convoy W.S.8B
escorted by Exter
Cairo & 8 destroyers
(sailed Clyde 22nd May)

Through the voice-pipes and telephones came cries of "Fire!" and the agonized screams of wounded men. The torpedo officer reported that the 4-inch ready-use ammunition was exploding, and Briggs could hear the UP rockets going up, both evidently triggered by the fire.

Captain Kerr ordered the 4-inch-gun crews to take shelter and told the fire and damage control parties to keep well away until all the ammunition had exploded. At 6 A.M., Holland ordered, "Turn twenty degrees to port together." This was passed to the flag deck, and a blue pendant was hoisted on the yardarm. At last the two British ships could bring their after turrets to bear, which would give them the overwhelming superiority of eight 15-inch guns and ten 14-inch guns to their opponent's eight 15-inch guns.

Within seven minutes, Hood had fired twelve four-shell salvos, Prince of Wales nine five-shell salvos, and Bismarck had just fired her fifth four-shell salvo. Now, as Hood turned, the guns of her X turret roared out, but for some reason, those of Y turret remained silent. Then Briggs saw a blinding flash sweep around the outside of the compass platform, and its occupants were once again thrown off their feet. The ship jarred, then slowly listed to starboard. Through the voice-pipe, the helmsman reported, "Steering's gone, sir," to which Captain Kerr calmly replied, "Very good. Change over to emergency steering." Hood righted herself, but then began to list alarmingly to port.

As she continued to list, those on the compass platform realized that she was not going to come back. Some of the occupants made for the port and starboard doors; others tried to get out by breaking the reinforced glass windows. There was no panic among the men, only fear. Commander S. J. P. Warrand stood aside for Briggs to leave first. The young signalman looked back to see the vice admiral slumped in his chair with a look of total dejection.

Something unforeseen had occurred. The blinding flash that had swept around the compass platform had been a huge sheet of flame, which had evidently risen up between the after funnel and the mainmast through a boat deck already weakened by the preceding fire. It had rent the ship in two and sent a mass of debris high into the air. By the time Briggs had managed to climb down the ladder to the admiral's bridge, the sea was swirling around his legs. It was now a matter of survival.

⊷ ⊷ ≤♦≥ ⊷ ⊷

Action midshipman of the watch was eighteen-year-old William Dundas, to whom fell the responsibility of using the sextant that was directed onto *Prince of Wales* and reporting to the officer of the watch whether she was approaching too near or falling behind.

Dundas was standing not far from Ted Briggs on the compass platform when *Hood* was hit. He saw bodies, some dismembered, falling from *Hood*'s spotting position above him—the result, he believed, of *Bismarck*'s fourth salvo of shells hitting it without exploding. And after the fifth salvo, wreckage started raining down again.

When *Hood* began listing heavily to port, Dundas found himself unable to leave the compass platform by the door through which Briggs got out. He was therefore obliged to kick in the window on the starboard side and escape that way, spraining his ankle in the process. Even so, he found himself being dragged down under the water before suddenly popping to the surface like a cork.

Dundas managed to drag himself onto one of the many Carley rafts that were floating about amid the debris in the oil-covered water. The rafts had been stowed on the weather deck and were automatically released by the water pressure when the ship sank. Here and there, patches of oil were blazing, and there was a real risk that he might be engulfed by the flames. The stern of *Prince of Wales* was visible as she fought in desperate rear-guard action, but he knew that by the rules of naval warfare, a ship in action could not stop to pick up survivors. It became apparent that he was not the only survivor, for Briggs too had managed to climb aboard a raft.

Dartmouth 2nd XV rugby team 1940. Dundas center sitting.

JEANNIE MCLEAN

"The Bismarck *Action: The Destruction of HMS* Hood."

ARTIST JOHN HAMILTON (COURTESY MRS. BETTY HAMILTON)

Although both Briggs and Dundas had gone into the sea from the starboard side, Briggs had emerged on the port side. He realized, therefore, that he must have gone right under the ship. This experience was akin to the old-fashioned naval punishment of keelhauling, and how he survived is a mystery, but one medical possibility is that his larynx went into spasm at the shock of being submerged in the ice-cold water, which prevented water from entering his lungs. This is the same primitive reflex that allows a baby to survive for a short time the shock of being submerged in water. Alternatively, there may have been a pocket of air that kept him alive.

Able Seaman Robert E. Tilburn.
BRIAN TILBURN

It was exactly four years to the day since the twenty-year-old Robert Tilburn had joined the navy. Now he was stationed at *Hood's* port after 4-inch antiaircraft gun.

As soon as *Bismarck* began to return the British ships' fire, the antiaircraft crews on *Hood's* upper deck were ordered to take cover in the recreation space at the base of the control tower. Everyone obeyed except four of the men, Tilburn among them, who lay down on the deck and exchanged banter to relieve the tension. An enemy shell then hit the forward antiaircraft gun, causing the 4-inch ammunition and UP rockets to explode and a fire to start. Fanned by the wind created as *Hood* steamed along at 28 knots, the fire was so intense that it was impossible to get near it, let alone put it out. A shell from the next salvo hit the recreation space where their shipmates had gone to take shelter, and another explosion killed two more of Tilburn's companions.

As *Hood* began heeling to port, he discarded as much of his gear as he could and jumped onto the forecastle, only to be washed away by a great wave. *Hood's* bows were rising into the air, and she was sinking by the stern. Tilburn was to owe his survival to his prowess at swimming—his father had been champion swimmer of the police force at his hometown of Leeds in Yorkshire. Now, in the water by *Hood,* he struck out and, but for his strong swimming, he would have been sucked under by the sinking ship. The mast hit the water before he had gotten clear, and his legs became entangled in a yard and an aerial wrapped around his feet, dragging him under. He slashed at his boot with a knife and kicked it off, then shot to the surface in time to see *Hood's* bow pointing skyward in a final salute before she slid down beneath the waves. As *Prince of Wales* carried on the fight, he saw flames and smoke leap up from *Bismarck,* and it cheered him to see that she had been hit.

Tilburn swam toward some piles of wreckage and saw the other two survivors. It was impossible for him to get near their rafts, as the wreckage was surrounded by oil, patches of which were burning. After what he estimated to be an hour, he could stand the cold no longer. The waves were washing over his head, and the water temperature was only a few degrees above freezing. He decided to take a chance and swam toward one of the rafts. "If I am going to die," he told himself, "I want company."

The three men attempted to stay together by hanging on to the ratlings of each other's rafts. Dundas, the only one of the three who was an officer, realized that if they were to fall asleep, they would quickly succumb to the cold, so to keep them all awake, he had them sing "Roll Out the Barrel" and other familiar songs over and over again.

More than an hour had passed when Tilburn shouted that he could see an airplane. It was a Sunderland flying boat. But though they yelled for help and splashed about with their hands, the pilot failed to see them.

Dundas then suggested that each should tell the story of his escape from *Hood*. Inevitably, however, the time came when their cold and stiffened fingers were no longer able to grasp the ratlines and they drifted apart. Dundas continued singing. Then he suddenly shouted, "There's a destroyer coming along! She's seen us!" "It's *Electra*!" screamed Briggs, who recognized the pennant.

The ship cut her engines and steered toward them. The crew onboard tossed them ropes and rigged scrambling lines. Dundas sang one last chorus of "Roll Out the Barrel," and after an ordeal that had lasted four hours, the three men were hauled up. *Electra*'s crew removed the men's frozen clothes, swathed them in blankets, and gave them each a tot of rum. The ever cheerful Dundas said to *Electra*'s first lieutenant as he was hauled up onto the main deck, "Sorry I can't salute, sir. I'm afraid I've lost my cap." Then he collapsed.

Flying Officer Pinhorn, a pilot of a Hudson aircraft of the RAF Coastal Command, had observed the sea battle and had given *Hood*'s last known position. This had enabled HMS *Electra* to reach the scene fifteen minutes earlier than it would otherwise. But for this, the three men's lives might well have been lost.

＋⇥ ⇤≢⇥ ⇤＋

Having hoped to find hundreds of survivors out of *Hood*'s company of over fourteen hundred men, the destroyers searched the area until 9 P.M., but there were no more to be found. Others might conceiv-

ably have managed to float and swim away from the dying *Hood,*
through the debris and the burning oil. However, the shock of being
suddenly immersed in ice-cold water, together with the fact that they
would have been unable to get at and inflate their life jackets, which
they wore routinely *under* their Burberrys, made their chances of survival minimal.

Other ships also searched. Petty Officer E. Hephen was on a V
and W destroyer (a class of ship so called because the names of all the
vessels in that particular class began with either a *V* or *W*), HMS
Windsor, on convoy duty in the area. After the action, they searched
for a while until U-boat warnings caused them to have to depart.

CHAPTER 12

Prince of Wales
Fights On

PRINCE OF WALES, STATIONED ON *HOOD'S* STARBOARD QUARTER, had only just turned to port with Vice Admiral Holland's signal and was now obliged to reverse rudder quickly and alter course to avoid the wreckage of the sinking *Hood*. She had just fired her ninth salvo, but this maneuver forced her to waste precious seconds and disrupted the pattern of her gunnery.

Up until now, *Hood* had drawn the enemy's fire, leaving *Prince* in comparative peace. Now that she was gone, *Bismarck* and *Prinz Eugen* were able quickly and with only a small alteration of gun bearing to concentrate solely upon *Prince* and direct the combined fire of both their secondary and main armaments on her at a range of 18,000 yards. Soon *Prince* was hit with four 15-inch and three smaller shells.

With *Hood* lost, Captain Leach decided to switch on his radar. The Type 284 was defective, but he was able to use the Type 281 air-warning set to determine the enemy's range, though it is uncertain with what success. As far as his optical rangefinders were concerned, he was encountering the same problems as *Hood* had faced. The views from the enormous 42-foot rangefinder at the back of A turret and the 35-foot rangefinder at the back of B turret had both been obscured by spray, so Captain Leach was obliged to open fire on a range obtained with the smaller rangefinder situated on her control position.

Despite the heroic efforts of the civilian engineers from Vickers in rectifying faults as they arose, *Prince* was averaging only three-gun salvos instead of five, and toward the end, her salvos were falling short and wide.

At 6:03 A.M., the range was down to 14,100 yards. *Prince of Wales* had fired a total of eighteen salvos from her main 14-inch fore and aft turrets and five from her secondary 5.25-inch armament. Captain Leach now made the decision to break off the action. He altered course to 160 degrees, and as his ship hauled away under cover of smoke, heeling over in the process, her 14-inch after turret jammed, putting all four of its guns out of action. The enemy ships made no attempt to follow her. Unknown to Captain Leach, he had acted just in time, for his ship had come within range of *Prinz Eugen*'s torpedoes, and her captain, Helmuth Brinkmann, was on the point of opening fire.

Captain Leach's reasons for breaking off the engagement were threefold. First, the mechanical problems with the guns had prevented them from producing their full output; second, his ship had only just reached the stage of being reasonably fit to take part in service operations; and third, he saw no likelihood of a decisive concentration in favor of the British, though it was a possibility later when reinforcements arrived. Under the circumstances, therefore, he did not consider it wise to continue single-handedly the engagement with the two German ships, both which likely were at the peak of their efficiency.

Prince of Wales's plotting officer did not realize that his ship had been hit until blood began trickling down the bridge voice-pipe and dripped onto his chart. Splinters from one of the exploding shells blinded Lt. Esmond Knight, actor, artist, and ornithologist, who had half hoped he might have the chance of seeing some arctic bird life during the voyage into northern waters. Another explosion caused torrents of scalding water to be released onto the survivors on the bridge and onto men on the signal deck below.

During the encounter, *Prince* had sustained considerable damage. A 15-inch shell passed through her compass platform, killing or wounding everyone on it. Captain Leach was injured when he was thrown from one end to the other, and both he and his chief yeoman of signals were knocked down and momentarily dazed. The shell fortunately failed to explode until it emerged from the far side of the bridge structure. A second shell struck the starboard foremost 5.25-inch director, and a third hit the aircraft crane and shattered both wings of the aircraft, which had to be jettisoned. A fourth pierced the ship's side below the waterline and the armored belt, passed through several bulkheads, and came to rest in the diesel dynamo room but failed to explode. In consequence, 400 tons of water entered the stern compartments, which reduced the ship's speed to 27 knots. This shell was only discovered and defused later, when the ship docked at Rosyth. An 8-inch shell from *Prinz Eugen* penetrated the after superstructure and came to rest on the upper deck but did not explode. Another partially exploded on the lower armored deck aft, and a third struck the ship's side aft and also only partially exploded above the armored deck. *Prince's* casualties were two officers and eleven men killed and one officer and eight men wounded.

Bismarck, however, did not escape unscathed. The first evidence that something was amiss came from a British Sunderland flying boat from Iceland, which had made contact with the cruiser HMS *Suffolk* just before the action began. Having witnessed the destruction of *Hood,* she approached *Bismarck* to identify her. Although the plane came under antiaircraft fire, the pilot was able to report that *Bismarck* was leaving in her wake a broad track of oil.

Bismarck had been hit twice by 14-inch shells from Prince of Wales. One had penetrated the port oil bunker, causing a serious oil leak as well as contamination of the battleship's fuel-supply system. The second struck the side armor amidships, causing flooding of a dynamo and a boiler, which reduced the ship's maximum speed by 2 knots. The damage was sufficient to cause Admiral Lutjens to abandon his proposed foray into the Atlantic and to make for St. Nazaire for repairs. Prinz Eugen continued with the original plan, however, and later in the day slipped away from her consort and disappeared into the broad Atlantic Ocean.

At the time of Hood's sinking, Rear Admiral Wake-Walker, in the cruiser Norfolk, was ten miles to the north and approaching at 28 knots. With the loss of Vice Admiral Holland, it now fell to him to take command of the remaining ships. He fully approved of Captain Leach's decision to break off the action, and at 6:30 A.M., signaled his intention of maintaining touch with the enemy. Prince of Wales was to remain astern of him as part of a shadowing force but should make no attempt to engage the enemy until they could be reinforced. Wake-Walker therefore ordered Captain Leach to open out to a distance of ten miles on a bearing of 110° so that the rear admiral would have his battleship to fall back on if attacked.

⊷ ⇥⬥⇤ ↢

Admiral of the Fleet Sir Dudley Pound had read the accounts and studied the charts relating to the operation against Bismarck. He informed Admiral Tovey that he proposed to bring both Rear Admiral Wake-Walker and Captain Leach to trial at court-martial, as they had failed to engage Bismarck during her run south after the action with Hood, turning away from the enemy instead.

After a distinguished career, during which he had served as flag captain of the battleship HMS Colossus at Jutland, Pound in his later years had gained something of a reputation for acting impulsively and inappropriately against officers whom he considered to have been in

Admiral of the Fleet Sir A. Dudley P. R. Pound, First Sea Lord and Chief of Naval Staff. HMSO

dereliction of their duty. In fairness to him, however, he now suffered from arthritis of the hip, and the resulting pain and insomnia often made him irritable. He had also developed a tumor on the brain, which eventually proved fatal.

Tovey was appalled at Pound's accusations. Had the British ships persisted with the action after *Hood* was lost, this could have had disastrous consequences, causing further loss of ships, or could have driven the enemy westward and away from his main battle fleet, which eventually caught up with and destroyed the enemy. Because of Wake-Walker and Leach's decision, the cruisers *Norfolk* and *Suffolk* and the battleship *Prince of Wales* escaped unscathed and survived to fight another day.

Rear Admiral Wake-Walker had been shadowing some fifteen miles astern of the enemy when battle was joined. Because of Vice Admiral Holland's imposed radio silence, however, he was not kept informed of the battle cruiser fleet's rapid approach and thus on their arrival had not been in position to participate in the ensuing battle.

Pound instructed Tovey to visit *Prince of Wales* at Scapa Flow on her return from the Denmark Strait to convey the grim news of

Pound's charges. Tovey signaled back that he would obey if given a direct order, but in the event that the two men were court-martialed, he would haul down his flag as commander in chief and appear at the trial as the "prisoners' friend." After that, said Tovey, "I heard no more about it." In the end, Captain Leach was awarded a Distinguished Service Order.

CHAPTER 13

The End of
Bismarck

EVEN WHEN THE CAPITAL SHIPS WERE FIRING AT EACH OTHER, ROYAL Marine George Jackson heard nothing of it, closed up in his gun turret in the cruiser HMS *Suffolk*. The first he knew of *Hood*'s sinking was when his captain announced it over the intercom. *Hood* was held in reverence by the Royal Navy—she was *the* ship—and Jackson had been greatly impressed by the shiny timber planking of her immaculately scrubbed quarterdeck when he had last seen her at Scapa Flow.

At 6:19 A.M., on the morning of May 24, nineteen minutes after the sinking of *Hood*, *Suffolk*, which had the enemy in sight, opened fire at the close range of 19,500 yards. Jackson's X turret and the Y turret were unable to bear, but a total of six salvos were fired from the A and B turrets, the last at a range of 12,400 yards. At 6:25 A.M., *Prince of Wales* signaled *"Hood* sunk," and at 6:37 A.M., Rear Admiral Wake-Walker, who had now assumed command in the absence of Vice Admiral Holland, gave the order for the destroyers *Electra, Echo, Icarus,* and *Achates,* which were away to the northeast, to search for survivors. At 7:57 A.M., *Suffolk* reported that *Bismarck* had reduced her speed and appeared to be damaged, and soon afterward a Sunderland flying boat from Iceland signaled that *Bismarck* was losing oil.

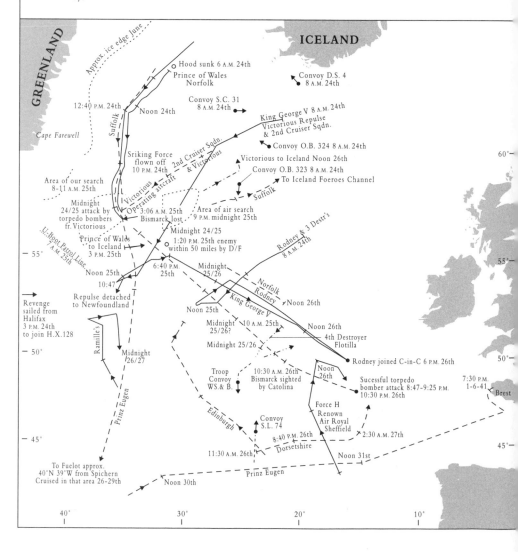

The Pursuit of Bismarck
(Second Phase)
8a.m. 24th—11:30p.m. 26th May 1941
Note: The tracks of main units only are shown

British:

Battleships & Fleet	———————▶
Cruisers	– – – – – – – ·
Carriers(detached)	– · – · – · – · – ·
Destroyers	– – – – – – –
Aircraft	·············
Convoys	●–▶

German:

Bismarck	– – – – – – – ·
Prinz Eugen(detached)	– – – – – – – ·
U-Boot	··················

GREENLAND

ICELAND

Approx. ice edge June

Hood sunk 6 A.M. 24th
Prince of Wales
Norfolk

Convoy D.S. 4
8 A.M. 24th

Convoy S.C. 31
8 A.M. 24th

12:40 P.M. 24th

Noon 24th

King George V 8 A.M. 24th
Victorious Repulse
& 2nd Cruiser Sqdn.

Cape Farewell

Suffolk

Sriking Force
flown off
10 P.M. 24th

2nd Cruiser Sqdn.
& Victorious

Convoy O.B. 324 8 A.M. 24th

Victorious to Iceland Noon 26th
Convoy O.B. 323 8 A.M. 24th
To Iceland Foeroes Channel

Area of our search
8-11 A.M. 25th

Victorious Operating aircraft

Suffolk

Midnight
24/25 attack by
torpedo bombers
fr. Victorious

3:06 A.M. 25th
Bismarck lost

Area of air search
9 P.M. midnight 25th

U-Boot Patrol Line
7 A.M. 25th

Prince of Wales
to Iceland
3 P.M. 25th

Midnight 24/25
1:20 P.M. 25th enemy
within 50 miles by D/F

Rodney & 3 Destr's
8 A.M. 24th

— 55°

Noon 25th

10:47

6:40 P.M.
25th

Midnight
25/26

Norfolk
Rodney

55° —

Revenge
sailed from
Halifax
3 P.M. 24th
to join H.X.128

Repulse detached
to Newfoundland

King George V

Noon 25th

Noon 26th

— 50°

Ramille's

Midnight
26/27

Midnight
25/26?

10 A.M. 25th

Noon 26th
4th Destroyer
Flotilla

50° —

Midnight 25/26

Rodney joined C-in-C 6 P.M. 26th

Troop
Convoy
WS.& B.

10:30 A.M. 26th
Bismarck sighted
by Catolina

Noon
26th

Sucessful torpedo
bomber attack 8:47-9:25 P.M.
10:30 P.M. 26th

7:30 P.M.
1-6-41
Brest

Prinz Eugen

Force H
Renown
Air Royal
Sheffield

2:30 A.M. 27th

— 45°

Edinburgh

Convoy
S.L. 74

8:40 P.M. 26th

45° —

To Fuelot approx.
40°N 39°W from Spichern
Cruised in that area 26-29th

11:30 A.M. 26th

Dorsetshire

Noon 31st

Prinz Eugen

Noon 30th

| 40° | 30° | 20° | 10° |

Norfolk, Suffolk, and *Prince of Wales* continued to track the enemy throughout the day, despite mist and *Prince's* frequent alterations of course. They sent out frequent enemy reports, which were picked up by Admiral Tovey's battle fleet, which was still 360 miles to the east.

At 6:14 P.M., *Prinz Eugen* managed successfully to detach herself from *Bismarck* and head undetected for the French port of Brest. At 6:40 P.M., *Bismarck* emerged from the mist on *Suffolk's* starboard beam and opened fire with seven salvos at a range of ten miles. *Suffolk* immediately returned fire but damaged her bridge in the process. Three minutes later, *Prince of Wales* was also in action, and three minutes after that, *Suffolk* again opened fire with both A and B turrets. The enemy replied with three salvos, which fell short or aft of the ship. *Prince* then fired three more salvos. In this engagement, *Suffolk* had fired sixteen broadsides, totaling sixty-five rounds, and the efforts of Jackson and his colleagues to get X turret operational had not been in vain.

Shadowing continued throughout the evening, and at one minute past midnight on May 25, torpedo bombers from the aircraft carrier *Victorious,* which had sailed with Tovey's battle fleet from Scapa Flow, attacked *Bismarck.* One hit was recorded.

At 3:06 A.M., contact with the enemy was lost when *Bismarck* made a change of course of almost 360 degrees. Luck was with the British, however, because Admiral Lutyens gave his position away by breaking radio silence and sending a signal to the German Admiralty. Meanwhile, Admiral Tovey's battle fleet, and Vice Admiral Sir James Somerville's Force H, which included the aircraft carrier *Ark Royal,* the battle cruiser *Renown,* and the cruiser *Sheffield,* which had sailed from Gibraltar, were closing in.

At 7:10 P.M. on May 26, fifteen Swordfish aircraft from *Ark Royal* attacked *Bismarck,* one torpedo hitting amidships and another striking and jamming the rudder. With British ships converging on her from all directions, including battleships and cruisers detached from convoy duty, *Bismarck* stood no chance. Against her were ranged four battleships, two battle cruisers, three heavy cruisers, two aircraft carriers, ten light cruisers, and twenty-one destroyers. In the end, it was the cruiser *Dorsetshire* that sank *Bismarck* with torpedoes, at 10:40 A.M. on May 27.

Suffolk, which with *Norfolk* had done her work well, had stood off from the action while the final drama had unfolded. She was then commissioned to go to the North Atlantic to search for the ship which it was assumed would be waiting there to supply *Bismarck.* In this she was unsuccessful, however.

PART THREE

The Postmortem

CHAPTER 14

The Boards of Enquiry

SOON AFTER THE SINKING OF *HOOD*, A BOARD OF ENQUIRY, presided over by Vice Admiral Sir Geoffrey Blake, was set up to try to determine the cause. No shorthand notes were taken during the proceedings. Midshipman Dundas was the only one of the three survivors to be interviewed. Positioned as he had been on the compass platform, he was able to confirm that there had been no hits on the forward part of the ship and little noise from the explosion.

The Board concluded that the probable cause of the loss of HMS *Hood* was direct penetration of the protection (armor) by one or more 15-inch shells at a range of 16,500 yards, resulting in the explosion of one or more of the after magazines.

This, however, did not satisfy the director of naval construction (DNC), Sir Stanley Goodall, who in July 1941 drafted his own report. He pointed out that the ship's magazines were nowhere near the mainmast, where the explosion was actually observed. The forward bulkhead of the 4-inch magazine was 64 feet abaft the center of the mainmast, and its after bulkhead about 115 feet abaft. Had this 4-inch magazine exploded and caused the X magazine to blow up, the Y magazine would have done likewise, and the aft bulkhead of Y magazine was even farther from mainmast, 180 feet away. Therefore, an explosion in the location observed could not be explained by an explosion of the after magazines. The DNC proposed an alternative explanation: that it was an explosion of one or more of *Hood's* above-deck torpedo warheads that caused her to sink.

In view of the DNC's report, Adm. Sir Dudley Pound, the first sea lord, ordered that a second Board of Enquiry be set up in which all possible witnesses from all ships present at the action would be interrogated. Rear Admiral H. T. C. Walker presided, and the board included experts on explosives and naval construction.

Witnesses from HMS *Suffolk,* which was twenty-eight to thirty miles away, described seeing arise from *Hood* "a pillar of orange flame which rose about 800 or 1,000 feet into the air." This was followed by a cloud of very dark smoke. Rear Admiral Wake-Walker, from HMS *Norfolk,* which was about fifteen miles away, described a fire burning in the after part of the ship with a clear reddish flame. This appeared to die down and then increase. There was then a big explosion, with a high sheet of flame shaped like a fan or inverted cone, surmounted by dark smoke. Chief Petty Officer French, from *Prince of Wales,* said that the middle of the boat deck appeared to rise before the mainmast.

Dundas had been on the compass platform at the chart table and in no position to see aft. He did, however, see a mass of brown smoke as the ship began her final, fateful list to port. As he scrambled uphill and climbed out one the windows, he noticed the officer of the watch climb through another window. When he was halfway through, the water came up underneath him, and the next thing he knew he was swimming. He heard no blast louder than that of the ship's own guns firing.

R. E. Tilburn had been on the boat deck, but because he was lying down, his view was restricted. As the ready-use ammunition exploded (eighty rounds of 4-inch ready-use ammunition were stowed in light type lockers on the boat deck), it sounded like "a big Chinese cracker." When in the water, Tilburn saw steel tubes approximately fifteen feet long and one foot in diameter, which the board believed were the crushing (energy-absorbing) tubes from the antitorpedo bulges just below the waterline, which might indicate that the ship had broken in half.

Ordinary Signalman Briggs remembered hearing the senior gunnery officer saying, "She has been hit on the boat deck and there is a fire in the ready-use lockers," to which the vice admiral replied, "Leave it [attending to the fire] till the ammunition is gone." Immediately after the explosion, Briggs heard the officer of the watch state that the "compass had gone" (gyro-repeater on the compass platform). There "was not a terrific explosion at all regards noise."

The technical witnesses believed that the "balls of fire" seen in the explosion must have been either partially ignited cordite charges or projected oil fuel taking fire in the air.

This second Board of Enquiry, which reported on September 12, 1941, stated that "the fire was not in itself the cause of, and was distinct from the explosion that destroyed the ship." It doubted whether a torpedo warhead explosion could have been the cause, because this would have produced "an all round almost instantaneous flash" and not the high column of flame of appreciable duration seen by so many witnesses. Nor was there any noise heard that was "compatible with that of TNT detonation or explosion." The board concluded: "The sinking of *Hood* was due to a hit from *Bismarck*'s 15-inch shell in or adjacent to *Hood*'s 4-inch or 15-inch magazines, causing them all to explode and wreck the after part of the ship. The probability is that the 4-inch magazines exploded first."

It is significant that immediately after the circulation of the second Board of Enquiry's report, the UP rocket apparatus was removed from every ship that had been fitted with it. Also, the upper deck torpedo armament similar to that on *Hood* was removed from the battle cruiser HMS *Renown,* and armor protection was increased in a score of other battleships and battle cruisers. One question still remained: Had the Boards of Enquiry ascertained the truth?

The Concept of an Immune Zone (I.Z.)

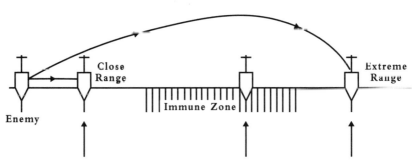

Inside the I.Z. the enemy shell has a high velocity and a low trajectory and is therefore more likely to strike and penetrate the belt.

Within the I.Z. the shell has insufficient velocity to penetrate the belt, and if it strikes the deck it does so obliquely and therefore loses much of its penetrating power.

Outside the I.Z. the shell will be plunging. It is therefore more likely to plunge down through the deck.

CHAPTER 15

Vice Admiral Holland's Tactics

VICE ADMIRAL HOLLAND WOULD HAVE BEEN FAMILIAR WITH THE concept of the "immune zone." The nearer a ship is to the enemy, the higher the velocity of the enemy's shells and the lower their trajectory. Too near, and the ship risks an enemy shell striking and penetrating its belt armor, as at that range the shell is more likely to strike the belt than the deck. However, the ship can also be endangered by being too far away from the enemy, and in a position where a shell fired with the guns highly elevated could plunge down vertically through the deck—and the maximum penetrating power of a shell is when it strikes the armor perpendicularly.

The immune zone is the area between too near and too far. For HMS *Hood,* the inner limit was defined as a range no closer than 12,000 yards, and the outer limit beyond 25,000 to 30,000 yards. For HMS *Prince of Wales,* the inner limit was 13,000 yards. If the ships fought the battle within the "immune zone," they were in comparative, not absolute, safety.

So was Holland within these boundaries when he fought his battle against *Bismarck?* To determine this, it is necessary to know the whereabouts of the four principal ships in relation to one another at

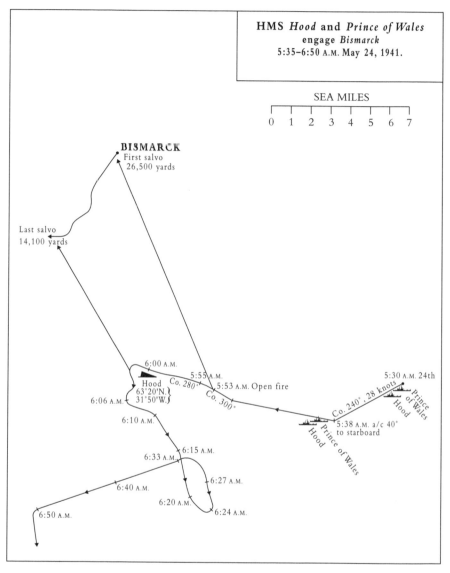

HMS *Hood* and *Prince of Wales*
engage *Bismarck*
5:35–6:50 A.M. May 24, 1941.

SEA MILES

0   1   2   3   4   5   6   7

BISMARCK
First salvo
26,500 yards

Last salvo
14,100 yards

6:00 A.M.
5:55 A.M.
Co. 280°
Hood   5:53 A.M. Open fire
63°20'N.}
31°50'W.}   *Co. 300°*
6:06 A.M.

5:30 A.M. 24th

Co. 240°, 28 knots
Prince of Wales
Hood

5:38 A.M. a/c 40°
to starboard
Prince of Wales
Hood

6:10 A.M.
6:15 A.M.
6:33 A.M.
6:40 A.M.   6:27 A.M.
6:20 A.M.
6:50 A.M.   6:24 A.M.

the various stages of the battle. But is this possible, when the large optical rangefinders in the forward turrets of the British ships were obscured by spray, so that the perceived ranges were determined by using the smaller, less accurate instruments in the control towers? Also, visibility may have been poor, as dawn had just broken, and the sun was still low in the arctic sky.

Hood's logbook lies at the bottom of the ocean and is unavailable for scrutiny. There does remain *Hood's* and *Prince of Wales's* Action Plot, as well as the personal record of survivor Ted Briggs, who was signalman on *Hood's* bridge. However, the information from these two sources should be regarded critically. The Action Plot is not drawn to scale and therefore gives a distorted picture, and recollections of figures given in the heat of battle may not always be reliable.

The stated range that *Hood* sent out at 5:35 A.M. in her enemy report when she first sighted *Bismarck* was seventeen miles. Even at this great distance of just under 30,000 yards, all three capital ships were within range of one another's guns and would have been in danger from plunging shell fire. With the sighting of *Bismarck,* Holland, who was steering at 240°, accordingly altered course at 5:38 A.M. to 280° in order to close the range. Then, at 5:49 A.M., he made another 20° turn to starboard. At 5:53 A.M., he opened fire. The range this time was given by the Action Plot as 26,500 yards, by the Admiralty's Board of Enquiry as 25,000 yards, and by Ted Briggs as 13 miles (22,800 yards). Of these differing figures, the range stated by the Board of Enquiry is perhaps likely to be the most accurate, and if so, then *Hood* and *Prince of Wales* were becoming less and less vulnerable to plunging enemy fire every minute.

The question now is whether Holland's squadron was still within the immune zone at the time of *Hood's* sinking. The range then, according to the Board of Enquiry, was 16,500 yards, and this figure tallies well with the Action Plot diagram. Therefore, Holland was still a comfortable 4,500 yards inside what should have been the comparative safety of the immune zone.

The position of the two British ships in relation to the enemy was important, because on this depended both the target area they presented and the number of guns they were able to bring to bear. For the British ships, the ideal situation was to keep the target they presented to the enemy to a minimum, to have the target presented by the enemy be a maximum, and to have all British guns bearing. For *Hood,* to take an extreme situation, a beam-on approach, with *Hood*

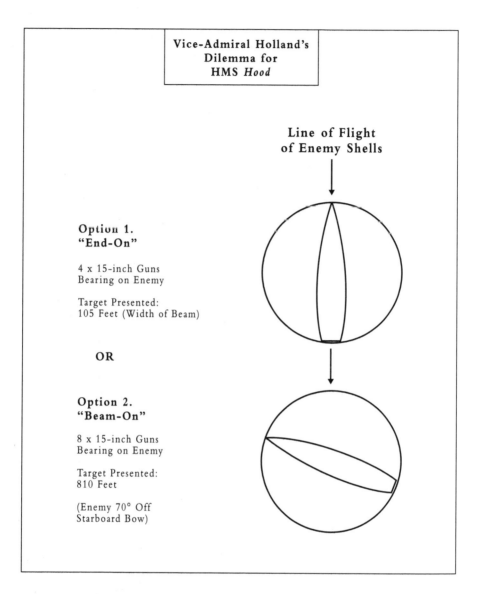

**Vice-Admiral Holland's
Dilemma for
HMS *Hood***

**Line of Flight
of Enemy Shells**

**Option 1.
"End-On"**

4 x 15-inch Guns
Bearing on Enemy

Target Presented:
105 Feet (Width of Beam)

OR

**Option 2.
"Beam-On"**

8 x 15-inch Guns
Bearing on Enemy

Target Presented:
810 Feet

(Enemy 70° Off
Starboard Bow)

square on to the enemy, would have enabled her to bring all eight of her 15-inch guns to bear, but she then would have presented her entire length of 860 feet as a target. Conversely, an end-on approach, with her bow pointing directly toward the enemy, would have enabled her to bring only the four guns of her two forward turrets to bear, but the target she presented would have been only the 104-foot width of her beam.

Between 5:49 and 5:55 A.M., Holland was steering 300°, with the enemy approximately 25° off his starboard bow. In these relative positions, the British ships presented an effective target to the enemy of roughly 40 percent of their lengths. In this position, however, only the guns of *Hood's* two forward turrets were bearing.

With the object of bringing into play his two additional after turrets—or, in naval parlance, to open A arcs—Holland now made two turns to port. However, his first 20° turn, made at 5:55 A.M., exposed far more of *Hood's* length to the enemy than had previously been the case, and in turning another 20° to port at 6 A.M., the exposure amounted to virtually the whole of *Hood's* 860-foot length. It was in this act of turning that *Hood* received her mortal blow.

Because Holland had required that *Hood* and *Prince of Wales* attack together, the same considerations about target area presented to the enemy and gun-bearing capability applied equally to both ships.

Why did Vice Admiral Holland require that the two British ships attack in close order—in other words, with *Prince of Wales* at a distance of a mere 800 yards on *Hood's* starboard quarter? It may be that with his insistence on radio silence, he was reliant on flag signals to coordinate the movements of his two ships. Should visibility deteriorate to the extent that the flags could not be seen, he would then lose control of the situation. He was only too well aware that the weather had already tricked him once, when the enemy was engulfed in a snowstorm and disappeared off the shadowing cruisers' radar screens.

Also, by adopting the close-order approach, Holland was acting in the manner prescribed in the Admiralty's manual of *Fighting Instructions,* drawn up in 1939 by Admiral of the Fleet Sir Dudley Pound.

Holland denied his squadron the use of radio, as he wanted to conceal his position and surprise the enemy. But in doing so, he also denied himself the support of Rear Admiral Wake-Walker's two shadowing cruisers and the six escorting destroyers.

＊＋＝＋＊

As his ship broke up, Vice Admiral Holland sat slumped in his admiral's chair in utter dejection, seemingly oblivious to the noise going on all around him, and making no attempt to move as it slowly sank under him. Perhaps his last thoughts were of his wife, who was anxiously awaiting news back at home. Or did the sudden brutal realization that he had failed in his mission totally overwhelm him? For a sailor, his ship is his home. As *Hood* lurched sickeningly, Holland knew that his ship—his home, even though he had been aboard her for only a matter of days—was irretrievably lost, and because it was closed up for action stations, there would be few if any survivors.

Admiral of the Fleet Sir Dudley Pound, the first sea lord, proclaimed after the battle in a memorandum that "no blame attaches to the Vice-Admiral [Holland] commanding the Squadron, the Captain [Kerr] or anyone else." Nevertheless, in the years that followed, people have wondered whether the outcome would have been different had Holland acted other than as he did.

Holland's predecessor, Rear Adm. Sir William Whitworth, was in favor of an end-on approach, so as to present the enemy with the smallest possible target. His commander in chief, Admiral Tovey, was of virtually the same mind when he suggested a permitted maximum deviation of only 10° from end-on, and after the sinking of *Hood,* Tovey allegedly told the first sea lord that he wished Holland "had been steering in more." In fact, Holland had every opportunity to attack end-on, because the enemy ships were well within his gun range, and there was no danger that they would outflank him. That is apparent from *Hood's* and *Prince of Wales's* Action Plot. But for some reason, Holland chose not to do so, and instead exposed progressively more of *Hood* to the enemy until, with his final turn, virtually her whole length was exposed, rather than merely her beam (which was only 12 percent of her length) that would have been the case had he attacked end-on. *Prince of Wales* had the same percentage increase of exposure.

Had Vice Admiral Holland and Captain Leach maintained the course they had adopted at 5:49 A.M., which was 300°, or had they turned even farther to starboard *toward* the enemy, instead of turning away, they still would have had an advantage in heavy gunpower—nine forward 15 inch guns (discounting the one gun of *Prince* that was able to fire only a single round) against *Bismarck*'s eight. They also would have presented the smallest possible target, and the enemy ships would then be crossing in front of the British ships' bows (in naval parlance, crossing their T), exposing the whole of their length as a target.

Holland's decision to attack in close order reflects the fact that despite his undoubted abilities, he lacked battle experience. The tactics he used tended to be based on the Admiralty's *Fighting Instructions,* which he preferred to follow rather than use his own best judgment. Had the two British ships attacked from different directions, the enemy ships would have been forced to divide their fire. Instead, when *Hood* was hit and disabled, Captain Leach had to put *Prince*'s rudder hard over to avoid the wreckage, costing him valuable seconds during which he could have been firing at the enemy. And now, having sunk *Hood,* the enemy ships were able to quickly shift targets to *Prince of Wales* by altering their gun bearings only a few degrees.

Holland, again with the object of achieving surprise, failed to make use of *Hood*'s Type 284 gunnery radar set until a very late stage. This had been fitted just two months previously and was known to give accurate results on a large target such as a battleship at a distance of up to ten miles. Ted Briggs stated that *Bismarck* and *Prinz Eugen* were picked up by *Hood*'s radar bods when the enemy ships were twenty miles away, but the radar was evidently not used to find the distance of the target. In retrospect, it can be argued that the radar would have been a most valuable aid to both Holland and Captain Leach, particularly in the heat of battle, when spray was flying over the forecastle and obscuring the lenses of the optical rangefinders.

Rear Admiral Wake-Walker believed that the Admiralty thought him lacking in offensive spirit, and this was confirmed by Pound's attempt to bring both Wake-Walker and Leach to trial by court-martial. However, Holland's insistence on radio silence meant that prior to the action, Wake-Walker was unaware of the battle cruiser fleet's intentions, though with his cruiser HMS *Norfolk* at a range of only ten miles, he would have known their disposition.

In conclusion, it appears that Holland's greatest mistake was attempting to bring his after turrets to bear (open A arcs), when he would have been better advised to steer toward the enemy end-on. The notion that ships as large as *Hood* and *Prince of Wales* could, in order to fire broadside, hope to expose with immunity the whole of their lengths to an enemy as powerful as *Bismarck* was unrealistic. Perhaps the more sensible notion of a ship going into battle end-on and using only the forward turrets had been in the minds of the designers of *Prince of Wales* when they situated six of her ten 14-inch guns forward and four aft.

PART FOUR

The Enduring Mystery of Hood's Loss

CHAPTER 16

Doubts Over
the Official Verdict

BOTH BOARDS OF ENQUIRY CONCLUDED THAT A 15-INCH SHELL from *Bismarck* struck *Hood* in or adjacent to her 4-inch or 15-inch magazines, causing them all to explode and wreck the after part of the ship. In their conclusions, however, they were careful to avoid venturing an opinion as to whether the offending shell had penetrated the side of the hull, known as the belt, or the deck.

According to the Boards of Enquiry, when *Hood* was sunk, she was at a range of approximately 17,000 yards from *Bismarck*. She was therefore well within the immune zone. A shell striking her at this range would have been traveling on a low trajectory and, statistically speaking, would have been more likely to strike the belt than the deck, even though *Hood's* deck was three times larger in surface area than the belt.

If such a shell *had* hit the belt, penetration would have been unlikely for the following reasons: *Hood's* belt protection was superior in strength to that of any other ship in the navy. Not only was it 12 inches thick, it was inclined at an angle of 12° to the vertical, which represented a virtual armor thickness of 13 inches, making it even stronger. This is why the inner edge of the immune zone for *Hood,* even though she was an old ship, was 1,000 feet closer to the enemy than for the newer *Prince of Wales.*

Hood *being attacked by Italian Regia Aeronautica bombers in*
the Mediterranean, July 1940. R. WAITING

Less likely, but not impossible, is that a shell may have struck the
deck. Such a shell would, however, have struck at an angle so oblique
that its penetrating capacity would have been reduced to as little as
30 percent.

Additionally, of the 15-inch shells that hit *Hood* and *Prince of
Wales* in the action against *Bismarck,* most, if not all, failed to explode
or did so only partially. Therefore, even if a shell, as suggested by the
Boards of Enquiry, had managed to penetrate through the armor and
into one of the after magazines, chances were that it had not
exploded.

Hood's two after 15-inch magazines were situated beneath the X
and Y turrets and above the shell-handling rooms, and each contained 125 tons of cordite wrapped in silk bags. The 4-inch magazine
was located beneath the admiral's quarters, between the X turret's
15-inch magazine and the engine room.

The combustion of cordite, so-called because it is produced in
cordlike form, is extremely rapid and produces huge high volumes of

gas. This instant provision of motivating power makes it an excellent propellant for shells, and quality control in its manufacture was of such a high standard that precision shelling, even at several miles' range, could be achieved.

Cordite is difficult to ignite, and once ignited, it burns slowly with a strong yellowish flame. It only burns explosively when strongly confined, as, for example, in a ship's magazine. It is so stable and so insensitive to shock that it cannot be exploded by a rifle bullet passing through it. The minimum temperature of the flash required to explode cordite M.D. is 2,374° Centigrade (4,305° F) , and there is no doubt that had a 15-inch shell exploded in one of *Hood*'s magazines, the result would have been a catastrophic explosion.

Nevertheless, there remains one flaw in the virtually identical "exploding magazine" conclusions of the two Boards of Enquiry. To understand it, one must go back twenty-five years to May 31, 1916, the Battle of Jutland, when Adm. John Jellicoe's British Grand Fleet was ranged against the German High Seas Fleet under Adm. Reinhard Scheer, and three British battle cruisers were lost in a single afternoon.

The first casualty was HMS *Indefatigable,* which was hit by shells from her German opponent *Von Der Tann.* An explosion occurred, followed by flames and sheets of thick black smoke. Debris was hurled into the air and the stricken cruiser turned over and disappeared beneath the waves.

The second was HMS *Queen Mary,* which was firing her eight guns broadside at the German battle cruiser *Derfflinger* when, at a range of 14,400 yards, the British ship was struck. There followed an explosion forward and a much heavier explosion amidships, which threw debris and a gigantic cloud of smoke high into the air. Observers said that the whole of the center of the ship appeared to collapse inward, and an instant later she disappeared.

The third was HMS *Invincible,* the flagship of Rear Admiral Hood. She was hit amidships by a 12-inch shell, also from the German battle cruiser *Derfflinger,* which ignited the two magazines of the

Bomb damage to Hood's *12-inch armored belt.* FRED WHITE

two midship turrets and caused a rapid succession of heavy explosions, which sent up an enormous amount of black smoke and broke the ship in half. The admiral was lost, along with 1,020 officers and men out of his company of 1,026.

The inadequate flashproofing of the turrets of these three World War I battle cruisers was what led to their downfall, but by the time HMS *Hood* was built, that problem had been corrected.

However, there was one difference between the sinking of these ships and the sinking of *Hood* that cannot be ignored: Whereas with the Jutland ships there were massive, loud explosions as one magazine went off and triggered the next and the next, with *Hood* there was no explosion whatsoever. Midshipman Dundas and Signalman Briggs, who were on *Hood's* bridge at the time, recalled no sound of an explosion at all, and Esmond Knight, who was observing from *Prince of Wales,* said, "I remember listening for it and thinking it would be a most tremendous explosion, but I don't remember hearing an explosion at all."

CHAPTER 17

Other Possible Causes

Over the years the cause of HMS *Hood*'s sinking has provoked endless speculation. Alternate theories have centered around the fire that started on the boat-deck, the above-deck torpedoes, or the possibility of hull penetration by a shell or a torpedo.

THE FIRE

Bob Tilburn, who was manning the port after 4-inch gun, insisted that the first hit on *Hood* was achieved by an 8-inch shell. This must therefore have been fired by *Prinz Eugen,* as *Bismarck* had no such armament, her next caliber down from 15-inch being 5.9-inch. Tilburn also stated that had this shell been a 15-inch, he in all probability would have been killed.

Cmdr. "Tiny" Gregson, who walked out onto the starboard wing of the compass platform to inspect the damage, said the hit occurred at the base of the mainmast, which was sixty-five feet distant from the nearest magazine, and started a fire. Ted Briggs, also on the compass platform, heard the screams of wounded and burned men echoing down the voice-pipes.

Lt. Esmond Knight, who had witnessed everything from *Prince of Wales* before losing his sight in the action, said about *Hood:* "The fire was on the forward part of the boat deck and spread immediately afterwards. It was a most enormous fire; it seemed to burst into flames so rapidly—high, licking red flames and dense, pitch black smoke. I remember thinking they would have a very hard job to put it out. It was so complete that it seemed to involve the after part of the ship almost." But Tilburn, who was closer and therefore in a better position to see what actually happened, stated categorically that the explosion had occurred at the base of the mainmast, which was situated at the after part of the boat deck.

Knight went on to say, "At the same time I think *Prinz Eugen* was firing some H.E. [high explosive shells], which was bursting in the air, bits of which were spraying into the water all around." It appeared to Knight that the enemy's shells were exploding just astern of *Hood,* and he failed to understand how the Germans could have set the fuses for so great a range. In reality, what he was seeing was the exploding ready-use 4-inch and pom-pom ammunition, and *Hood*'s own UP rockets, with their $9^{1}/_{2}$ tons of refills stored unsafely in light steel lockers that had been fitted in exposed positions on the boat deck. This would have contributed enormously to the blaze.

Knight was probably correct in believing that *Prinz Eugen* was using high-explosive shells. These contain the largest charge possible with the case of the shell still retaining sufficient strength to withstand the shock of being fired from the gun. They are intended for use against unarmored targets, in this instance with the object of disrupting the enemy's gunnery by destroying vital exterior mountings, such as rangefinders, directors, antennae, and fire-control equipment. They have little penetrating power. As *Prinz Eugen*'s 8-inch guns were firing at a distance well in excess of half of their maximum range, her shells would have been falling on *Hood* at a steeper angle than those fired by *Bismarck,* or in other words, describing a plunging trajectory.

Captain Leach, on *Prince of Wales,* described the fire as "a vast blowlamp," and certainly, with *Hood* steaming at 28 knots, the wind would have greatly fanned the flames. When *Hood* was hit again, many of the gun crews who had taken shelter in the aircraft hangar were killed.

The fire would certainly have consumed numerous boats, and also have burned its way through the unarmored boat deck to the wardroom kitchen, pantry, galley, and the wardroom itself, where there was a considerable quantity of flammable material, such as wooden tables, chairs, and pictures. It may also have traveled aft to the cabins of the flag lieutenant, the surgeon commander, and the engineer, and beyond this to the admiral's quarters, including cabin, bathroom, pantry, lobby, sleeping cabin, dining cabin, and day cabin. This accommodation would have contained unfireproofed material, dating from when the ship was constructed, and never upgraded. However, the two inches of armor at the level of the forecastle deck presumably would have prevented the fire from penetrating further downward into the torpedo, gunnery, or printing offices, the post office, and the secretary's writers' office, and to the numerous messes.

Might this intense fire on the boat deck have spread deep down into the ship through inlets and outlets open to the atmosphere? The existence of the gas citadel—a zone that embraces as many compartments as practicable for ventilation and intercommunication purposes, and includes all living spaces and all spaces occupied by men in action—makes this unlikely. All ventilation systems in the gas citadel are fitted with gas-tight flaps, by means of which their supplies and exhausts can be temporarily cut off from the atmosphere, as when a ship is in action. Fans recirculate the air inside the citadel and supply filtered air through special filtration units designed to keep oxygen and carbon dioxide at the levels necessary for physical and mental alertness.

Whatever the cause of the catastrophe that befell *Hood,* observations would seem to indicate that she broke in two. Her forward section reared up sharply before sliding back into the sea and disappearing, making it likely that the after part, which had less buoyancy, broke off and sank almost immediately. Might the fire have weakened the ship sufficiently to have caused this?

Because the lessons of the battle of Jutland were slow to be appreciated, *Hood*'s design always lagged behind the realities of contemporary naval warfare. This was why, when her keel was first laid down on May 31, 1916, work on her was suspended until September 1 in order for new design features to be incorporated.

The requirements for a battle cruiser were a high freeboard, which would ensure that the weapons could be operated in heavy weather without being drenched by water or spray, combined with a relatively shallow draft, which in the event of underwater penetration of the hull would mean that the pressure and therefore the force of the water entering the ship would be that much less and flooding more easy to control. In order to avoid sacrificing space needed to include all the required machinery and weaponry, this reduction in draft required a corresponding increase in length and beam.

In the case of *Hood,* however, by the time her final design was approved, not only had the requirements of shallow draft and high freeboard been almost completely sacrificed, but her displacement had increased to 41,200 tons, which was almost 5,000 tons above the original estimate. For this reason, *Hood* was always known as a wet ship—her stern was a mere seventeen feet from the waterline, and she tended to ride even deeper when traveling at speed, with her quarterdeck often awash.

Could *Hood*'s great length, combined with the facts that her structure had to bear the weight of two pairs of heavy 15-inch guns and turrets set 500 feet apart, and that she possessed one deck fewer than contemporary battleships in order to accommodate a greater length of machinery, have had a detrimental effect on her strength? Did the fire weaken an already strained spine sufficiently for her to break in two? These things are unlikely, for the following reasons. Her hull was divided by transverse bulkheads into twenty-five main watertight compartments. She had a double bottom, and her longitudinal frames, spaced about eight feet apart, were continuous over her length. In the upper part of the ship, additional strength was provided by the decks, which ran unbroken for her entire length. *Hood*'s design of longitudinal frames, transverse frames, beams, and decks all interlocked meant that, in effect, she had the strength of a giant box-shaped girder.

HOOD'S TORPEDOES

The second Board of Enquiry report addressed the question of whether *Hood*'s above-deck torpedoes could in some way have caused the loss of the ship. Its conclusion was that "although the explosion or detonation of the two [torpedo] warheads cannot be entirely excluded, this was not the direct cause of the loss of the ship."

Torpedo tubes, HMS Hood. FRED WHITE

The director of naval construction, Sir Stanley Goodall, who, with A. L. Attwood, had presided over *Hood*'s design, proposed an entirely different cause for the loss of *Hood* than the "exploding magazine" theory. He believed that the tragedy may have occurred when an enemy shell detonated her torpedo warheads in one of the pairs of above-water torpedo tubes. Goodall's predecessor as director, Sir Eustace Tennyson-d'Eyncourt, had fought a long and constant battle

Hood *firing a torpedo.* FRED WHITE

to have these fittings removed, on the grounds that their exposed position rendered the ship vulnerable.

Four 21-inch Mark IV torpedoes were kept in above-water tubes, two on either side at the base of the mainmast, and four reloads were slung from rails immediately overhead, all warheads being enclosed within a 3-inch armored box. Each warhead contained 515 pounds of TNT, and if a single one had exploded, this almost certainly would have been sufficient to have broken the ship's back.

TNT, short for trinitrotoluene, is a very stable explosive. But unlike cordite, it ignites at a relatively low temperature—about 250° C (482° F)—and disastrous explosions have occurred when large quantities have been involved in a fire, because rapid explosive decomposition occurs between 281° and 286° C.

An explosion of one or more of *Hood*'s torpedo warheads could have been triggered either by the shock of the concussion of an enemy shell hitting and exploding at the base of the mainmast where they were situated, or by the boat-deck fire raising their temperature to the critical ignition point for TNT of 250° C (482° F). But again, if a torpedo had exploded, why was there no explosive bang?

UNDERWATER PENETRATION

Hood was the first ship to have a comprehensive system of underwater protection incorporated form the design stage. Previously built ships were reliant on torpedo bulkheads only, or on embryonic torpedo "bulges," such as were built into the battle cruisers *Renown* and *Repulse*. On *Hood,* the bulge consisted of an outer air space, an inner buoyancy space, and a 1^1/2-inch-thick protective bulkhead. The buoyancy space was filled with sealed steel tubes known as crushing tubes, which were designed to absorb the force of an underwater explosion and distribute it over as large an area of the protective bulkhead as possible. The armored belt, which sloped 12° to the vertical, was kept inside the bulge structure in order to allow torpedo hits to vent upward into the atmosphere. The bulge covered only the length of the hull between the end turrets. There was no necessity for complete protection along the whole length, because it was estimated that with her watertight compartments, the ship could withstand the explosion of several torpedoes and still remain operational without serious loss of speed.

Hood's 12-inch-thick armored belt covered 562 feet of her length and was 9^1/2 feet in depth, of which 5^1/2 feet was above the water and 4 feet below. Between the forecastle deck and the upper deck, it was 5 inches thick; between the upper deck, the full 12 inches. Below this, the armor tapered to 3 inches. The torpedo bulge overlapped the belt up to the level of the main deck to give added protection.

There is no evidence to suggest that *Hood* was subjected to a torpedo attack by the enemy ships, and at the closest range at which she came to them, 17,000 yards, she was marginally outside the range of a torpedo anyway. It is possible, however, that one or more of *Bismarck*'s 15-inch shells, describing as it would have at that short range

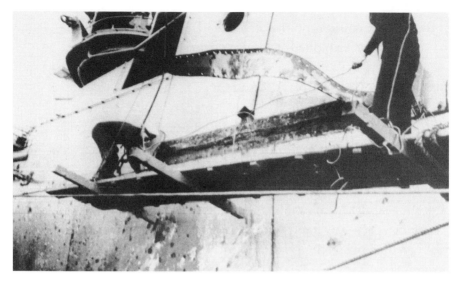

Bomb damage to Hood's *12-inch armor.* FRED WHITE

a relatively low trajectory, may have dived underwater and struck either the armored belt or the torpedo bulge. The chance of this happening would have been all the greater if the ship had been rolling away from the enemy at the time, because the bulge would then be more exposed, or if she were encountering large waves, the troughs of which would also expose more of her underside. But *Hood* was not prone to roll to any great extent except in extreme weather conditions, and she tended to cut through the waves rather than glide over them, as many a soaked crew member knew.

The bulge might have been sufficient to absorb the energy of the impact of a shell, particularly if, as occurred with many or all of *Bismarck*'s 15-inch shells, it either failed to explode or did so only partially. In the unlikely event that the hull was penetrated, would this have been sufficient to cause the great ship to break in two and sink in just a few seconds? The penetration and explosion of enemy shells undoubtedly would have caused one or more of *Hood*'s watertight compartments to flood, but her strength derived from the "box-girder" construction made it highly unlikely that this could have caused so sudden a catastrophic a demise.

A shell fired by *Bismarck* from $8^1/_2$ miles' range and penetrating the ship below the waterline would have been too low to enter a magazine, but it possibly could have entered one of the shell-handling rooms below. In that case, the flash produced by resulting detonation could have traveled upward and exploded the cordite. But if this happened, then again, why was there no bang of an explosion?

CHAPTER 18

Conclusion

THOSE WHO HAVE ATTEMPTED TO DEDUCE WHAT EXACTLY CAUSED the sinking of HMS *Hood* have tended to concentrate on *Bismarck* as the culprit. However, because of that ship's faulty shells and the fact that *Hood* was inside the immune zone when sunk, it seems unlikely that *Bismarck*'s primary armament could have been the cause. It is even more unlikely that her secondary armament could have been responsible, as this consisted of only 5.9-inch guns.

Unlike the guns of her larger and more powerful consort, *Prinz Eugen*'s 8-inch guns were being fired at over half their maximum range, so her shells would have described a steep trajectory and fallen down onto their targets more vertically. Although *Hood* was most vulnerable to plunging shells, it is virtually impossible that a shell of only eight inches in caliber could have penetrated through the decks to reach any of the ship's vitals, such as her magazines. But there was one part of *Hood* that *was* vulnerable to plunging shell fire, and that was her two funnels, the combined area of which, as seen from above, presented a target area of 600 square feet.

The probability of a shell going down one of *Hood*'s funnels may seem remote, but certain factors make this more likely than the other theories. The enemy had an advantage in that the fire on the boat deck illuminated the target perfectly, and *Prinz Eugen* was able to fire

From the siren platform, Hood's *after funnel showing protective cage.*

off salvos from her eight 8-inch guns at approximately twice the rate of *Bismarck,* which meant that during the time she was in action, she managed to loose off 179 rounds.

If a plunging 8-inch shell from *Prinz Eugen* did indeed go down a funnel, the flimsy wire cage that covered its top would have provided little resistance. The next thing the shell would have encountered as it fell would have been a grating, positioned in the vents at the level of the lower deck to protect the boiler room below. This grating, 5 inches in depth with bars ¹/₂ inch thick and set 2¹/₂ inches apart, probably was made of the same material as the deck itself—cemented armor of high-tensile steel with a high carbon content, rather than armor plate. Trials conducted in 1924 showed weaknesses in the supports of these gratings, and a new design was developed, but it is doubtful whether this was ever incorporated into *Hood.*

Prinz Eugen is known to have picked up the sound of the British ships at a range of twenty miles, using her passive sonar array. In the mistaken belief that she was to engage cruisers, she had high-explosive (HE) shells loaded.

The armor-piercing shell has a thick casing and reduced charge to ensure that it penetrates right down into the vitals of an enemy ship. An HE shell, on the other hand, has a thin casing and the highest possible bursting charge. So on striking the grating, even if the HE shell was incapable of piercing its armor, it may well have dislodged it from its supports, which were known to be inadequate. It then would have entered and exploded in one of the boiler rooms—a most vulnerable part of the ship.

As observers reported that a huge flame shot upward from between the after funnel and the mainmast, it seems most likely that such a shell went down the after funnel—the one adjacent to the burning boat deck. But could this have ignited the fuel oil?

Fuel oil will not ignite below a temperature of about 90° C (194° F). Above that, it will ignite only in the presence of a flame unless the temperature rises to 350° C (662° F), at which point the

Hood's *funnels.* FRED WHITE

Engine Room. FRED WHITE

oil will self-ignite. An explosion in a boiler room would have ruptured the six Yarrow small-tube boilers, which had a working pressure of 235 pounds per square inch. It would also have ruptured the 19-inch-diameter pipes that carried steam from the boilers to the turbines and, more importantly, have ruptured the fuel-oil heater, which preheated the fuel before it was pumped into the eight fuel-oil sprayers.

If the preheated fuel oil was being sprayed at high pressure from ruptured pipes into the confined space of a boiler room in the presence of shell flash, the result would have been ignition of the oil and an enormous buildup of heat and pressure. This pressure would have been constrained from traveling horizontally by the resistance of the watertight bulkheads fore and aft and of the armored belt on either side, and from passing vertically downward by *Hood*'s double-skinned hull. The pressure would have quickly risen as the gases built up and would have found its release by taking the line of least resistance up through *Hood*'s decks, which had already been weakened to some extent by the boat-deck fire. This might explain why there was no audible bang.

Thomas McLaren, whose aircraft had escorted *Hood* on her final voyage, had witnessed the sinking of a ship by this very cause: An explosive device had gone down her funnel. McLaren was part of the crew of a Lockheed Hudson aircraft in search of a merchant vessel that the Germans had disguised as a Red Cross ship but in fact was a troop carrier. They located the ship and then power-dived on it, releasing a 250-pound general-purpose bomb. McLaren, who was in the turret, saw the bomb drop. By a thousand-to-one chance, it went straight down the ship's funnel. A huge black plume of smoke with a small reddish glow in its center issued out skyward, and as the troops swarmed onto the decks, the vessel broke in two. As with *Hood,* there was no audible bang—merely a deep rumbling sound, followed by tremendous vibration in the air that the plane crew felt as their aircraft climbed steeply away.

The Search for
the Sunken *Bismarck*
and *Hood*

It was June 8, 1989. Aboard the ship *Star Hercules*, Skipper Robert Ballard watched a video screen that showed underwater details illuminated by searchlights and picked up by three video cameras mounted in the remote-control robot Argo, which was searching for the wreckage of *Bismarck*. Argo's movements were being controlled from another room by a team that included Ballard's son Todd. Suddenly he started, as the screen showed a huge gun turret lying upside down in the mud.

For ten days, they had been searching an area of seabed roughly 350 miles off the southwest coast of Ireland and dominated by outcroppings of underwater volcanoes. A moment's lapse of concentration on behalf of those who were controlling Argo, and the whole enterprise would end in disaster. But the transponders that they had placed earlier on the ocean floor enabled them to navigate the robot with absolute precision, and its sonar would give them ample warning of any obstacles lying ahead.

It had taken three hours for the robot to descend the three miles to the floor of an ocean too deep for the sun ever to penetrate. They had covered over three-quarters of the search area but found nothing. Could the coordinates, given by the ships involved in a battle that had taken place forty-eight years earlier and upon which Captain Ballard and his crew relied, be wrong? Ballard, however, was buoyed up by the fact that it had been one of his team from the Woods Hole Oceanographic Institution, Cape Cod, Massachusetts, who in 1985 had discovered the wreck of the *Titanic,* also using Argo. If they could do it once, he thought, they could do it again.

Now, as he stared at the gun turret on the screen, Ballard realized that its huge size could only mean one thing. He had found what he was looking for—*Hood's* old adversary *Bismarck.* And soon, there was the ship herself, sitting upright on the seabed, sharp and clear, not obscured in any way by barnacles or seaweed or severely corroded as would have been the case had she been sunk in warmer climes.

She appeared to have started a landslide as she slid down the slope on which she had fallen, and a section of her stern had become detached, presumably by the force of her impact with the bottom. Fore and aft, two enormous swastikas were visible. Where her four turrets had been, there remained only four huge, empty holes. The gaping hole on her port side amidships had probably been caused by a shell, as it was situated some distance away from the nearest cordite magazine. Her 1.5-inch and 5.9-inch guns appeared to be virtually intact, as did the rear gunnery control station.

Unlike *Bismarck,* which lies at roughly the same latitude as the French port of Brest, *Hood* was sunk at a latitude of 63°20', which is only 200 miles or so south of the Arctic Circle and on a level with the southern tip of Iceland.

A letter was published in *The Times* newspaper of London on December 18, 1998, by the American deep-sea explorer David L. Mearns, survey director of Blue Water Recoveries, Ltd. Writing from his company's base at Haslemere in Surrey, he spoke of a proposed expedition "to provide conclusive videographic evidence of the precise damage inflicted on *Hood* by *Bismarck.*" He stressed that he was "fully aware that the wreck of *Hood* is a war grave and that the Military Remains Act of 1986 protects her from unauthorised disturbance. The expedition, should it be funded, is intended only for confirmation purposes, and we have no plans to remove any artifacts or steel samples, even for scientific study." Mearns was by no means inexperienced in this field, having previously located the wreck of the *Derbyshire* in the China Sea some 800 miles south of Japan.

The reference to steel samples arises because there have been questions over the quality of the metal used in *Hood*'s construction. This had been mentioned in an article in *The Times* by Damian Whitworth nine days before, on December 9. Researchers, he stated, believed that there were similarities between what befell *Hood* and what befell the *Titanic*.

> The two ships were built at different shipyards and several years apart, but records show that they were constructed from the same kind of steel, supplied to both ships by the manufacturer D. Colville and Co. of Motherwell in Lanarkshire. The company no longer exists, but experts believe that if the metal was the same it could have been a crucial factor. Opinion is divided.
>
> Timothy Foeke, a metallurgist at the National Institute of Standards and Technology at Gaithersburg, Maryland, suggested last week that rivets recovered from the *Titanic* showed signs of corrosion. But others have suggested that the hull of the *Titanic* was brittle and when the iceberg hit it simply shattered.

Whether inferior-quality steel was used in *Hood* can be established only by collecting a sample and subjecting it to analysis. As far as the *Titanic* is concerned, current thinking is that because she struck the iceberg at an angle, the resulting gash in her side was so long and spanned so many of her watertight bulkheads that it was impossible for her to remain afloat. It can be said in retrospect that had her captain steered bow-on into the iceberg, she may have had a better chance of survival.

Just days before this book went to press, on July 23, 2001, David Mearns finally succeeded in his quest to locate the wreck of *Hood*. After six years of planning, the expedition, sponsored by Channel 4, found the wreckage at 2,800 meters below the Denmark Strait. The ship is in three main sections, with the bow lying on its side, the main section upside down, and the stern sticking up out of the seabed with its ensign-staff still intact. Artifacts such as the anchor chain, propeller, ship's bell, and rudder fixed on a turn to port are clearly visible.

On July 26, 2001 a memorial service was held in which Ted Briggs, the last of the three survivors of the *Hood* disaster, marked the place of the sinking by laying a wreath and, at the press of a button, releasing a bronze commemorative plaque to rest on the ocean floor alongside the ship's bow. Accompanying the plaque, encased in a clear pressure-resistant casing, is a special CD-ROM containing a Roll of Honor of those who lost their lives.

A Strange Coincidence

THE SUN CAST ITS DYING RAYS ACROSS THE PALM TREES AND SAND dunes of Portugal's Algarve. It was early in the 1960s, and Thomas McLaren, who had escorted *Hood* in his Lockheed Hudson aircraft on her final journey, and his wife Ethel, were staying in a hotel that was off the beaten track.

McLaren was pleasantly tired that day. While his wife visited the local shops, he had been fishing with the hotel manager. Thoughts of World War II were far from his mind.

After finishing their evening meal early, McLaren and his wife were relaxing in the piano lounge when they noticed a lady sitting on her own. She invited them to join her. Soon her husband returned from the bar and asked if he could buy them a drink. As he walked away, McLaren said, laughing, "My word, if ever I saw a sailor's roll, that is it!" On his return to the table, the man confirmed that he had indeed been in the Royal Navy.

Judging that they were about the same age, McLaren inquired, "Were you on any of the big ships?" The man replied, "Yes—HMS *Hood*."

McLaren, knowing that there had been only three survivors from the *Hood,* thought the man was pulling his leg. He asked the man if he could name the destroyers that escorted *Hood* on her final voyage. The man answered correctly. Astounded, McLaren asked, "What was

your job on board?" "I was on the bridge," he said, "as Action Midshipman of the Watch—manning the close radio set."

McLaren felt a tingling down his spine. "Do you remember
being escorted by an aircraft?" "Yes," said the man, "a Lockheed
Hudson." "And did you communicate with that aircraft?" asked
McLaren. "Did it request permission to come in close to take photographs?"

Now it was the other man's turn to be astonished. "How did you
know that?"

"I was the man you were talking to!" McLaren told him.

For a few moments, they stared at each other in disbelief. The
years rolled back, and they felt once more the brotherhood of men at
arms. For the remainder of that holiday, the two couples were virtually inseparable, and McLaren and Bill Dundas spent much of their
time reliving old wartime memories.

BIBLIOGRAPHY

"A Guide to Boldre Church." Lymington, England: Printwise, n.d.

Attwood, E. L. *The Modern Warship.* Cambridge: Cambridge University Press, 1913.

"Battle Summary No. 5: The Chase and Sinking of *Bismarck.*" Naval Staff History, Second World War, 1950.

Board of Enquiry Report. Controller of His Majesty's Stationery Office and Director of Public Records Office, London.

Bowditch, M. R. *Cordite Poole.*

Bradford, Ernle. *The Mighty Hood.* London: Hodder & Stoughton, 1959.

Breyer, Siegfried. *Battleships and Battle-Cruisers 1905–70.* London: Macdonald, 1973.

"Coastal Command." London: His Majesty's Stationery Office, 1942.

Coles, Alan and Ted Briggs. *Flagship Hood.* London: Robert Hale, 1985.

Friedman, Norman. *Battleship Design and Development 1905–1945.* Greenwich: Conway Maritime Press, 1978.

Grefell, Russell. *The Bismarck Episode.* London: Faber and Faber, 1948.

Hard, John. *Royal Naval Language.* Lewes, England: The Book Guild, 1991.

Kennedy, Ludovic. *Pursuit: The Sinking of* Bismarck. N.p.: William Collins, 1974.

Newton, R. N. *Practical Construction of Warships.* London: Longmans, Green and Co., 1955.

Padfield, Peter. *The Battleship Era.* N. p.: Hart Davis, 1972.

Parkes, Oscar. *British Battleships.* London: Seeley Service, 1957.

Preston, Anthony. *Battleships.* Manchester, England: Gallery Books, 1981.

Raven, Alan and John Roberts. *British Battleships of World War Two.* London: Arms and Armour Press, 1976.

Roberts, John. *The Battlecruiser* Hood: *Anatomy of the Ship.* London: Conway Maritime Press, 1982.

Roskill, S. W. *The War at Sea.* London: His Majesty's Stationery Office, 1954.

Schofield, Vice-Admiral B. B. *Loss of* Bismarck. Surrey, England: Ian Allen, n.d.

Scott-O'Connor, V. C. *The Empire Cruise.* London: Riddle, Smith and Duffus, 1925.

Stephen, Martin. *Sea Battles in Close-Up: World War II.* Surrey, England: Ian Allen, Ltd., 1988.

Thorpe, Sir Thomas E. *Dictionary of Applied Chemistry.* 1921.

The Times. London.

Von Mullenheim-Rechberg, Burkard Baron. *Battleship Bismarck.* Annapolis, Md.: Naval Institute Press, 1990.

Who Was Who 1941–1950. London: Adam and Charles Black, 1952.

INDEX

Page numbers in italics indicate illustrations.

Achates, 57, 107
Adelaide, Australia, 43
Admiral Hipper, 53
Admiral Scheer, 53, 56, 67
aircraft, 38–40
  Hudson, *60*
Almirante Cervera, 32, 33
animals, HMS *Hood* acquired,
  12–14
Antelope, 57
Anthony, 57
Arethusa, 57
Ark Royal, 109
attire, 80
Attwood, A. L., 135
Auckland, New Zealand, 44
Aurora, 57

Bailey, Admiral, 16
Ballard, Robert, 147
Ballard, Todd, 147
Bay of Biscay, 40
Bell, Ron, 91
belt protection, 127
Berwick, 67
Bilbao, blockade of, 32–33

Birmingham, 57
Bismarck, xiii, *50*, 52, 53–54, 68,
  71, 73, 75, 141
  damage to, 103–4
  engagement of, 79–90,
    92–100, 101–6, *118*
  failed attack on, 54
  HMS *Hood* comparison, 63
  leaving Bergen, *52*
  pursuit of, *93, 108*
  search for sunken, 147–48
  sinking of, 107–10
Blake, Geoffrey, 32–33, 113
Blue Water Recoveries, Ltd., 148
Board, Robin, *35*, 35–36
Boards of Enquiry
  first, 113–14
  flaws in verdicts of, 127–30
  second, 114–15
boats, 6, 64
  picket, 22, *31*
Bowhill, Frederick, 51
Briggs, Ted, 80, *91*, 91–92, 94,
  95, 97, 99, 119, 123, 130,
  131
  on HMS *Hood* sinking, 115

Brinkmann, Helmuth, 102
British Special Service Squadron,
    world cruise, 37–47
Bushell, Frederick Reeve, *37, 41*
    action station, 42
    duties of, 40, 41, 43
    on world cruise, 37–47

Cairo, 56
Cape Finisterre, 40
Cape Spartivento, Calabria, 80
Cape Town, 41
captain's messenger, 26
Carne, Chief Yeoman, 80
Castile Signal Station, 31
Christmas Island, 43
Church of St. John the Baptist,
    Boldre, *xv, xvi*
    Book of Remembrance, *xv*
Churchill, Winston, 52
codes
    international, 31
    naval, 31
cordite, 129
Cunningham, A. B. "Cuts," 29

Danae, 38, 47
Dartmouth ruby team, *96*
Dauntless, 38, 47
Dawon, Montague, xvi
Debric Fjord, 51
Denmark Strait, 56, 74
Denmark Strait, Battle of, 75–76,
    79–90, 91–100, 101–6,
    107–10
    first shots of, 75
Derbyshire, wreck of, 149
Derfflinger, 129
Dorsetshire, 110
Dragon, 38, 47

Dundas, William, 80, 95, *96,*
    98–99, 113, 114, 130, 152
Durban, 41

East London, 41
Echo, 57, 107
Electra, 57, 99, 107
Ellis, R. M., 56
engineer artificer (mechanic), 37
equator, crossing, 40
Exeter, 56

Fairey Flycatcher biplane, 38–40
Fancourt, Henry St. J., 54
Fegen, E.S.F., 53
Field, Frederick L. "Tam," 38
Fighting Instructions manual, 121,
    123
Firedrake, 32, 33
fleet
    battle cruiser, 57
    formation, 31
    Italian battle, 80
Fortune, 33
Franco, General, 32
Freemantle, Australia, 43
Freetown, Sierra Leone, 40
French, Chief Petty Officer, on
    HMS *Hood* sinking, 114
fuel oil, 143–45
funnels, HMS *Hood, 142, 144*
    shell going down, 141–46
Furious, 67

Galatea, 57
Gneisenau, 53, 54, 56, 68
Goddard, N. N., 54–55
Goodall, Stanley, 113, 135
Gotland, 54
Grand Canary Isle, 40

Grant, Fred, 16
Gregson, "Tiny," 80, 92, 131
gunnery, 88–90

Halifax, Nova Scotia, 46
Hamsterley, 32
Harud, Sayyad Khalifa ben, 41
Hephen, E., 100
Hermoine, 57
Hipper, 56
HMAS *Adelaide*, 44, 45, 46
HMS *Dainty*, sinking of, 9–12
HMS *Delhi*, 38, 44, 47
HMS *Dunedin*, 38, 44
HMS *Fishguard*, 37, 41
HMS *Ganges*, 30, 91
HMS *Glorious*, spring maneuvers,
    30
HMS *Hood*, 57, 58, 63–67
    Action Plot, 119
    aerial view of, *61*
    alongside South Mole at
        Gibraltar, *21*
    armament, 6–8, 64–67, *66*,
        88–90
    armor, 64, 127, 137
    being attacked in Mediter-
        ranean, *128*
    biplane on, 38–40
    Bismarck comparison, 63
    Bismarck engagement, 79–90,
        118
    boats, 6, 22, *31*, 64
    bomb damage to armor of,
        130, 138
    building of, 3
    chapel, 6
    control tower, *86*
    crew, 4

    description of, 3
    engine room, *145*
    engines, 6
    entering harbor in Malta, *xiv*
    excursions, 67–68
    exercises, *15*, 15–16
    final voyage of, xiii
    fire as cause of sinking of,
        131–35
    firing torpedo, *136*
    forward turrets, *86, 89*
    at Freemantle, *45*
    funnels, *142, 144*
    immune zone, 117
    laying down, *4*
    length and structure of, 134–35
    location of sunken, 148
    main passageways, 36
    mascot, 12, 43
    medical facilities, 6
    mission, 58
    name origin, 4
    negotiating Panama Canal, 12,
        45–46, *46*
    on-board torpedoes as cause of
        sinking of, 135–37
    on patrol, *23*
    pets, 12–14, *13, 14*
    pom-pom gun crew, *65*
    probable causes of loss of,
        113–15, 131–39, 141–46
    protective bulges, 8
    provisions, 4–6
    radar equipment, 123–24
    seamen's mess, 7
    search for survivors of, 99–100
    sectional drawings from blue-
        prints of, *5*
    seen from astern, *11*

shell going down funnel of,
    141–46
shoot, 87
sinking of, 92–99, 96
at speed, 82
spring maneuvers, 30
steel quality of, 149
steering compartment, 35–36
strange acquisitions, 14–16
torpedo tubes, 135
underwater penetration as cause
    of sinking of, 137–39
UP rockets, 65–67
utilities, 6
wardroom, 7
as wet ship, 134
witnesses of sinking of, 114–15
world cruise, 37–47
HMS Hood Association, 17
HMS Indefatigable, 129
HMS Invincible, 129–30
HMS Norfolk, 56, 67, 71, 73–76,
    124
    Bismarck engagement, 79–90
    in pursuit of enemy, 109–10
HMS Penelope, 9
HMS President, 20
HMS Prince of Wales, 57, 58,
    76–78, 77, 123
    Action Plot, 119
    Bismarck engagement, 81–90,
        92–100, 101–6, 118
    damage to, 103
    immune zone, 117
    in pursuit of enemy, 109–10
    radar equipment, 76–78
HMS Queen Mary, 129
HMS Renown, 16, 24, 109, 115,
    137

HMS Repulse, 38, 45, 46, 57,
    137
spring maneuvers, 30
HMS Sheffield, 73, 109
HMS Shropshire, 20
HMS Suffolk, 56, 68–73, 69, 74,
    75, 107
    armament, 69–70
    Bismarck engagement, 79–90
    in Denmark Strait, 70
    in pursuit of enemy, 109–10
    radar equipment, 69
    tracking the enemy, 72–73
HMS Windsor, 100
Hobart, Tasmania, 44
Holland, Lancelot E., 57, 79,
    79–80
    Battle of Denmark Strait and,
        81–90
    dilemma for HMS Hood, 120
    greatest mistake of, 124
    plan of action, 81
    tactics, 117–24
Honolulu, Hawaii, 45
Hood, Lady, 3
Hood, Samuel, 4
Hood, Horace Lambert, 3
Hudson aircraft, 60

Icarus, 57, 76, 107
immune zone, 116, 117, 127
Invergordon, unrest at, xiv
Italian battle fleet, 80

Jackson, George Bradford, 68,
    68–69, 72, 107
    duties of, 69
Jamaica, 46
Jellicoe, John, 44, 129
Jervis Bay, 53, 68

Jutland, Battle of, 129, 134

Kennedy, Charles Benjamin, *25*,
   25–27
  action station, 27
Kenya, 57, 68
Kerr, Ralph, 57, 80, *85*, 85–86
keyboard sentry, 26–27
King George V, 55, 57
Knight, Esmond, 103, 130,
   131–32
Kuala Lumpur, Malaya, 42

Leach, John Catterall, 77, 78, 84,
   106, 132–33
  Battle of Denmark Strait and,
   101–2
Lee, Able Seaman, 42
Leopold, Otto Eduard, Prince
  von Bismarck, 53
Lutjens, Gunter, 53, 56, 104

MacGregor, 32, 33
McLaren, Thomas E., 58–62, *59*,
   146, 151–52
McMullen, Colin, 87
Malaya, rubber estate in, *43*
Manchester, 57
maps
  Bismarck engagement, *118*
  Bismarck pursuit, *93, 108*
  world cruise, *39*
Mearns, David L., proposed
  expedition, 148–49
Melbourne, Australia, 44
midshipmen, 22
Mopan, 53

naval terminology, ix

Nevett, Bill, 92
Newell, Able Seaman, 71, *71*

Owens, Lieutenant Commander,
  80

Panama Canal, HMS *Hood* nego-
  tiating, 12, 45–46
Parker, Henry W., 38
Perth, Australia, 43
Phillips, A. J. L., 75
Pietermaritzburg, 11
Pinhorn, Flying Officer, 99
pom-pom gun crew, *65*
Port Swettenham, 42
Pound, A. Dudley, 81, 104–6,
  105, 114, 122
Prinz Eugen, xiii, 52, 71, 75, 131,
  141–43
  engagement of, 81–90, 101–6,
   109
  failed attack on, 54
  using high-explosive shells, 132

Quarrie, Ian, *19*, 19–24
  action station, 23
Quebec, 46

radar equipment
  HMS *Hood*, 123–24
  HMS *Prince of Wales*, 76–78
  HMS *Suffolk*, 69
RAF Coastal Command, Photo-
  graphic Reconnaissance
  Unit, 51
Ranson, W. H., *29*, 29–33
Robeck, John de, 37
rockets, UP, 65–67
Roosevelt, Franklin D., 52

Rotherham, G. A., 54–55
Royal Australian Naval College,
    Jervis Bay, 44
Royal Naval Volunteer Reserve
    (RNVR), 19, 35

St. John's, Newfoundland, 47
St. Lawrence River, 47
San Francisco, 45
Sawbridge, Captain, 16
Scharnhorst, 53, 54, 56, 68
Scheer, Reinhard, 129
seamen
    lost at sea, 16–17
    in tropical whites, *42*
Selassie, Haile (Emperor of
    Ethiopia), *11*
shells, explosive (HE), 143
signalmen, 30
Singapore, 43
Somerville, James, 80
"Song of HMS *Hood*," xi–xii
Spanish Civil War, 32
Stanbrook, 32
Star Hercules, 147
steel samples, 149
Suckling, Flying Officer, 51–52
Sumatra, 43
Suva, Fiji, 44
Swan River, Australia, 43
Sydney, Australia, 44

Tenerife, 40
Tennyson–d'Eyncourt, Eustace,
    135–36
Thurn, John I., 38
Tilburn, Robert Ernest, 63, 65,
    67, *97*, 97–98, 99, 114, 131,
    132
The Times, 148, 149

Titanic, 148, 149–50
torpedoes, HMS *Hood*, 135–37
Tovey, John C., 54, *55*, 55–58,
    78, 105–6, 122
Trincomalee, 42
Troop Convoy WS 8B, 55
Tuxworth, Frank, 91

Vancouver, 45
Victorious, 57, 109
Von Der Tann, 129

Wake-Walker, Cedric, 73
Wake-Walker, Christopher, 73
Wake-Walker, William Frederic,
    73–74, 74, 104, 105, 107,
    124
    on HMS *Hood* sinking, 114
Walker, H. T. C. "Hookey," 21,
    26, 114
Warrand, S. J. P., 80, 94
Wellington, New Zealand, 44
Western Samoa, 44
White, Fred, *10*, 17
    on watching sinking ship, 9–12
Whitworth, Damian, 149
Whitworth, William, 68, 122
Woods Hole Oceanographic
    Institution, 148
world cruise, British Special Ser-
    vice Squadron, 37–47
    itinerary, *38*
    map of, *39*
    statistics, 47
Wright, Yeoman, 80
Wyldbore-Smith, Lieutenant
    Commander, 80

Zanzibar, 41